HOW TO BUY AND RENOVATE A COTTAGE

HOW TO BUY AND RENOVATE A COTTAGE

Stuart Turner

Kogan
Page

Dedication

To my bank manager – for his continuing interest

Copyright © Stuart Turner 1982, 1987

First published by Patrick Stephens Ltd in 1982
under the title Buying and Renovating a Cottage;
this second revised edition published in 1987 by
Kogan Page Ltd, 120 Pentonville Road, London N1 9JN.

British Library Cataloguing in Publication Data

Turner, Stuart
  How to buy and renovate a cottage.———
  2nd ed.
  1. Dwellings ——— Remodelling ——— Amateurs'
  manuals
  I. Title
  643'.7   TH4816

  ISBN 1–85091–283–1
  ISBN 1–85091–284–X Pbk

Printed and bound in Great Britain by
Anchor Brendon Ltd., Tiptree, Essex

Contents

Introduction

The *Oxford Dictionary* I won on a coconut shy (it was either that or a goldfish) defines a cottage as a 'labourer's or villager's small dwelling; small country residence', while a Second World War song claimed that:

> *There'll always be an England,*
> *While there's a country lane,*
> *Wherever there's a cottage small,*
> *Beside a field of grain.*

So a key word when considering cottages seems to be 'country'. Nowadays you find town properties described as cottages and fetching high sums, but most of this book is about fairly small traditional places, well away from towns; I suspect this is what many people have in mind when they hanker after a cottage.

I hope you will forgive a little autobiography because I suppose I need to establish my credentials for writing a book like this. After starting married life in a small flat near Stoke on Trent (we all have our problems), my long-suffering wife, Margaret, and I then had ten different addresses in the same number of years. Our homes included flats and small bungalows, which we remodelled; two new houses built to our design; a caravan for six months while building went on around us; semi-derelict cottages and finally our present house which is a hotch-potch of a mid-thirties bungalow, linked to an old barn via a bedroom/kitchen bridge which we added.

Some years ago we—or at least our bank—bought a cottage at Coxwold in Yorkshire which was converted from a doctor's surgery. Later, the bank added a second cottage in Suffolk, which we totally renovated. Encouraged to further madness by the success of these two projects, we went hopelessly over the top and bought a dilapidated row of three cottages to convert near Bury St Edmunds, selling the Yorkshire cottage to pay for the work (having let it for holidays for some years). And if all that paints us as rural Rachmans then it is a false picture because it was all done on a very slender shoestring.

Although I once made a life-sized papier maché model of Sue Lawley from old copies of the *Radio Times*, I claim no great manual dexterity, so this is not really a DIY book, more a pratical guide on how to deal with estate agents, builders, architects, planners and so on. And above all, how to avoid the many pitfalls in renovating a cottage. All based on hard experience (I have the scars to prove it).

Finally, I must thank Peter Clarke, Roger Neville, Fred Hamlin, Valerie Morley, Mark Swift and Jill Reynolds for their valuable help with this book; the errors are all my own work.

Stuart Turner

1

Finding a Cottage

Do you dream of a cottage in the country with a thatched roof, a twirl of smoke lazing from the chimney and roses round the door? All for around £10,000? Forget it. If there *is* such a place, it certainly won't be going for £10,000. But don't despair because if you search hard enough you may still be able to find a cottage of some sort to renovate and, of course, many conversions done in the forties and fifties are now ready for a second wave of attention. According to a fairly recent government survey, almost a fifth of houses are still below standard and an incredible one million lack some of the basic amenities—hot water, a toilet or bath.

So it is worth searching. But first, stop, think and plan. And the first step in your planning should be to consider *why* you want a cottage. Will it be to live in, or retire to? As a second home or an investment?

Incidentally, to avoid accusations of male chauvinism I'd better make it clear that although I may refer to men throughout this book, most of the comments apply equally to women. With women increasingly independent and mobile, they form an important house-buying segment (as I was saying to my wife only the other day as she was cleaning my shoes). But whatever your sex, this first stage of your planning is something which I can't help you over. For every plus for a cottage, such as a rural position, there is a minus, such as no drains. Only you can decide if you really do want to take on the challenge. All I can say is that we have found it exhilarating and worthwhile.

Location

If you *have* convinced yourself that you are not daydreaming but really do want a cottage, then proceed to the next stage of your planning, which is to decide *where*. And here, do keep travel costs in mind in your decision making. Travelling a long way to and from work each day will leave the breadwinner/s too tired to mow lawns while, if a weekend cottage is so far away that you arrive late on a Friday evening and have to leave to drive back early on a Sunday afternoon, the novelty will quickly wear off. Do you want to live near relatives? Do you want a smaller house in your present area? Do you want to live at the seaside? If so, it may be a bleak house in the winter. The locals may call the air 'bracing', which actually means that you have to brace yourself at 45 degrees to walk along the prom with an independent air. If you are buying a cottage for holiday letting, there will be less wear-and-tear if it is inland because you will get fewer children than at the coast.

Your own age will affect your choice of area; for instance, being near a school is ideal when you have young children, possibly a pain when you have retired. If you plan to retire to a particular place, owning a second home there for a few years before doing so is an excellent way of establishing if you really like the area. But even discounting Welsh holiday home fires as the work of extremists, don't be too suprised if 'the locals' in some areas take time to accept you. If you consider that in the Lake District for instance, nearly a third of houses in choice areas are second homes then you can appreciate why locals get a bit uptight, particularly if winter turns some places into ghost villages. It also explains why there are political rumblings against second homes from time to time.

If you are a town dweller, remember you may find a totally different style of living in the country: no street lights, no launderette, no Chinese take-away. But to compensate: a better sense of values.

Having clearly thought through your reasons for wishing to move to a cottage and having established roughly where you want one, draw up your own individual checklist, considering such things as:

- Do you need easy access to shops, to a library, to public transport? Keep in mind what transport you have and how mobile you are likely to be as you get older.
- What are the school policies in particular areas?
- Are there local doctors, dentists, hospitals?

Finance

Having established why you want a cottage and roughly where, and having prepared a checklist of your particular wants, next decide roughly how much you can afford to pay. Money is covered in more

Figure 1 (Above) and Figure 2 (Below). *This cottage was first renovated by turning a third bedroom into a bathroom then, later, an extension was added at the rear. An additional soakaway would improve the appearance by allowing the diagonal drainpipe to run vertically down the cottage.*

Figure 3. *A challenge! A dormer window has collapsed and water has badly damaged the wall below.*

detail in Chapter 5 but at this stage of your planning you must have some idea of your financial position. Above all in your budgeting *allow plenty for contingencies*. Something unexpected is bound to crop up in renovating a cottage and do keep in mind that renovating will not necessarily be cheaper than buying a newer property (almost certainly the reverse) although at least you may be able to do some of the work yourself, and at your own pace.

However much your back-of-an-envelope calculations frighten you, don't rent a place if you can avoid it. If you are compelled to move (say, because of a change of job) and you can't find exactly what you want, then buy something 80 per cent suitable as a base while you look around and get to know the area (you'll need an understanding wife, of course, because this will mean two upheavals). In such circumstances it makes sense to buy something conventional and 'safe' so that you will be able to sell quickly when you have found your cottage.

Are you sitting pretty in a nice warm company house that goes with your job? You have my sympathy. Try to buy, not rent, property so that you get on the property ladder as soon as you can because, with inflation, what seems expensive today may not tomorrow and, provided you buy in a sensible area, a cottage should be a reasonable long-term investment. You may get more immediate satisfaction from antiques or vintage cars, but I doubt it. Nor can I see the same satisfaction in collecting cheese labels or stamps (admittedly I can't see rising damp or gardens to dig either).

Although the revenue from letting a cottage may not be all that great, what else can give you the same capital gain as property? Investing in a young artist? The art world is a bigger jungle than property. Dealing in the options market? You would need to devote most of your time to it, as you would dabbling in shares. I know the crazy boom years have gone, perhaps forever, but if you buy sensibly then I am convinced property owning is still worthwhile. But enough financial philosophising. Jot down the rough value of your present house, less estate agent's fees, legal fees, and any outstanding loans or mortgages; deduct removal costs and any oddball items you can think of. Is there anything left? Congratulations. That is roughly the total you have to cover a deposit and fees on a cottage.

Searching

Having got a rough idea of your financial ceiling (and do remember those confounded contingencies) decide what you are looking for. Don't be too rigid. You may set out with very clear ideas, then change them as your search progresses, but do jot down some fairly firm guidelines—such as how many bedrooms, whether you want a garage

Figure 4. *The second cottage from the left, with the repaired roof, proved an ideal first venture into cottage ownership.*

etc—because the more you plan, the better buying job you will do. Mind you, despite the emphasis throughout this book on planning, I must admit that we bought our first cottage on impulse. We were on holiday near York, happened to drive through Coxwold and saw a 'For Sale' sign outside a cottage, and fell in love with the place. We couldn't afford it (we had an overdraft at the time) but took a deep breath, found a friendly finance company and went in over our heads. The state of deep shock wore off after a few weeks and thereafter we never regretted our purchase.

Having settled how much you can afford, what sort of accommodation you need and roughly which area, you should now refine your search. Get hold of guide books, preferably not ones just describing churches and stately homes because you are unlikely to be living in them (if you are then thank you for buying this book, Your Grace). There is really a need for Bad Guides pointing out faults in places—the traffic jams, the noisy factories and so on. Take a holiday in an area if you are thinking of moving some distance so that you can decide if you really like it, but remember that a place may have a distorted appeal if you have the comfort of an hotel as a base.

When driving round an area, pencil notes on your map—particularly if a certain village appeals; if one doesn't then put a firm cross through it to remind you not to bother with anything in that area. Use pencil so that you can clean up the map from time to time, and do get good maps—Ordnance Survey ones are the best. Some estate agents, though not enough, give map references of properties which make them easy to find. Never use out-of-date maps; they may not show new roads, and you may waste time searching for a jasmine-covered cottage to find it fronts a motorway spur.

It is almost impossible to get a proper feel for an area without the mobility of a car. If you are stuck with public transport it will severely restrict just how much viewing you can do, so consider hiring a car for a day when you are down to a shortlist of places. Incidentally, do consider other motorists when viewing cottages. You can be a menace on the roads if you stop suddenly or veer across the road to view something. Log any traffic bottle-necks on your map.

The more you search around, the more you will get used to the feel of villages and an idea of prices. Have a pad and pencil to jot down notes and estate agents' phone numbers from signboards. Take a vacuum flask and emergency rations; house-hunting can be tiring and you will be more alert if you are fed and watered. Buy every local newspaper you can find and when you call at village shops to buy papers, ask the staff if they know of anywhere for sale. Study newsagents' windows; we once found a flat from a postcard in one. Even if you don't find a property, you may get names and addresses of gardeners, handymen and so on for later.

When you get back to base—and if that makes it sound like a military operation well, a search should be planned with some precision—anyway, when you get home, read the local papers from cover to cover, they may alert you to plans for power stations or airports. Above all, study estate agents' advertisements in the papers. We found one cottage tucked away at the end of a string of details for expensive houses:

LISTON, Nr LONG MELFORD
AN END-OF-TERRACE BRICK COTTAGE SET IN A DELIGHT-
FUL RURAL POSITION OPPOSITE THE CHURCH, 3 bedrooms,
2 reception rooms, scullery, garden.

I'd just got home after driving for hours round East Anglia, viewing countless places and was totally depressed because I hadn't found anything remotely in our price bracket, when I saw that ad. Half-heartedly I went to see it, and found a conventional cottage at the end of a terrace of four. As it was surrounded by beautiful countryside and opposite a superb church we stopped looking any further and made an offer which was accepted.

Figure 5. *The estate agent's advert describing this cottage as in a delightful rural position proved accurate. A break in the diagonal drainpipe caused damp inside on a bedroom wall, a common problem.*

While you are searching, chat to policemen as well as farmers (who will be well aware of the value of places so don't expect to buy any bargains from them). Talk to milkmen, talk to postmen and leave notes through likely letterboxes. If you find a derelict or unused property, but can't locate the owner, then write to, or phone, the local council. I suppose you could try advertising in the 'wanted' columns of local papers for a cottage although I've had no success with this method. Take *Dalton's Weekly* and *Exchange & Mart*. The former has more property in it, but the latter sometimes includes a few gems and is useful as a guide to material costs when you start renovating. Monthly house magazines concentrate on new properties and are of little use for cottages, other than for estate agents' names and addresses; the magazines *The Traditional Home* and *The Period Home* are worth taking, not for estate agents but because they have advertisements from people offering special windows, thatching, timber treatment and many other things you may need.

Estate agents

Using local newspapers and the Royal Institution of Chartered Surveyors' lists (published annually and usually available at solicitors) get on every possible estate agent's books. The more agents' particulars you receive, the better appreciation you will get of an area and of prices. Keep an eye on the agents who handle large farm estates because they may dispose of farm cottages too. Look in estate agents' windows and leave notes through their letterboxes if they are closed. DIY house-selling shops have sprung up and new schemes are regularly announced to cut across traditional selling methods (if nothing else these goad agents to improve their standards) but you are still most likely to be dealing with traditional estate agents and if you have never bought or sold a house before, and this is your first experience of them, then a whole new tapestry of life opens before you. An estate agent may give you a form to complete by ticking various boxes to indicate your requirements, but this is unlikely to cover exactly what you are looking for in a cottage and, from the particulars you will be sent, you may wonder if some agents ever look at their forms. But persevere, and remember that the response you get from an agent may depend on how well you brief him, so if you are absolutely opposed to living on a busy road, get this written in bold letters on your form. Estate agents get their commission from the *seller*, so although they may be perfectly friendly do remember that they are not acting for you in any transaction. Estate agents never seem liable for anything and they take little responsibility, as you will see from the careful clauses on their sales particulars. If you are new to an area, bear in mind that it has been known for agents to wheel and deal themselves. The Estate Agents Act requires them to declare an interest if an agent, employee or nominee is buying, but there are still ways and means . . . .

If you are viewing a property and think of a clever idea for a conversion, don't gush about it to the estate agents. I did this once and found that the place was sold next day to a friend of the agent; it may have been a coincidence but 'my' conversion was being done just a few weeks later.

If you have a degree in oriental languages or Esperanto, you may be able to understand estate agents' jargon, otherwise you are in for some disappointments. What their particulars *don't* include is more important than what they do. If a cottage sounds idyllic, that is the one next to a pig farm or with an electricity pylon in the back yard. You will find estate agents give words a whole new meaning:

Interesting	= bizarre
Compact	= tiny
A certain amount of renovation	= no roof
Period	= no hot or cold water
Scullery	= not much of a kitchen
Fitted kitchen	= the kitchen has a cupboard
In need of decoration	= derelict

If a cottage is described as 'unique' then be *very* cautious.

Agents quote maximum room dimensions, which can be misleading because a 15 ft x 10 ft room will be quite small if five of the 15 ft form a window bay, while what sounds like a large room may turn out to be an awkward L shape.

The phrase 'grants may be available' often appears in particulars for places needing work; don't let this lull you into a state of euphoria because the asking price may well have been jacked up accordingly.

You will also see the phrase 'or near offer' on agents' particulars from time to time, which may mean that they are open to a lower bid, so haggle. Similarly, if the price has been crossed out and another one written in, it may mean the place is sticking, so ask how long it has been on the market. If a cottage has already been sold when you stumble across it, or sold 'subject to contract', check again in a few weeks' time because sales can fall through (we found one this way).

Bright estate agents may well have video films of properties but if not, study photographs in agents' particulars with some care. If a photo shows snow on the roof of a property being sold in mid-summer, it may mean it has been on the market for some time and if sales particulars show a fine photograph of the *back* of a cottage, the front probably faces a sewage farm.

Viewing

You will often be turned loose with the keys to view a cottage on your own although, reasonably enough, you may be accompanied if there is any furniture in the place. Agents often have arrangements, when they are closed, to leave keys for collection at local hotels or garages, leaving you to push them back through their letterboxes later. You will find you can prod around empty places quite happily, studiously ignored by neighbours unless you ask them for specific advice; burglars must have an easy life.

If neighbours are out in their gardens, chat to them about the area. For instance, ask if the Red Arrows practise formation flying overhead every week. If you meet vendors while viewing, beware of 'deals' to bypass an estate agent and cut out his commission; it could cause litigation later between the agent and the vendor which could involve you.

Be serious in your viewing. Don't just prod around other people's homes for an afternoon's entertainment. Many trades attract people like this; car salesmen call them 'tyre-kickers'. Ask 'why are you moving?' Remember that the reason for selling may be that the seller has got wind of a new development in the next-door field—so ask neighbours as well as the vendor.

To save time, plot your viewing route with care before setting off. Code the sales particulars with A, B, C and so on then pencil the same letters on the map in the appropriate places. Plot the shortest route round the letters on the map, sort the sales particulars into that order—which may be E, A, D, C etc—then put them on to a clipboard. Scribble comments on the sales particulars as you leave a cottage because impressions will blur if you view a lot of places one after another. Note if there is room to extend into the garden. Is it possible to split a room into two? You will often find in older cottages that one bedroom leads into another; if so, is there room to put in a new wall to make a separate room? Whenever possible, draw a rough floor plan when viewing because this will help you to picture a place when you are ruminating on it later.

Does a cottage 'feel' right? Somehow or other, the one for you will make you feel at home in it. Don't go overboard for one oddball feature, such as a cute chimney, if the rest of the place is quite unsuitable. Don't let a beautiful view blind you to major problems with the cottage itself because once you are living there you will be looking at the crack in the wall or the ghastly chimney, not at the view all the time. Similarly a large garden may look splendid when viewing but be a millstone when you are installed. An old cottage surrounded by modern box bungalows can itself look out of place so avoid something like this.

You will probably want to avoid traffic noise, so take care if you are only able to view at weekends because traffic patterns and factory smells may be different during the week. Is the road in front of the cottage 'adopted'? In other words, is the local authority responsible for its maintenance? If not, pause before getting neighbours together to spend enough on the road to bring it up to a state where the local authority will take it over because the work could be expensive. Another cause for pause is that if you make up an unmade road, it may become a short cut for people going to work, trying to dodge traffic jams; holes in an unmade road can act as sleeping policemen.

I don't know whether you have enough power to control the elements but if so, view in the rain. View at any time that is unglamorous. View during school times to see how noisy it is. View when local factories are working to test if there are noises or smells. Are there any gypsy encampments in the area? If, like me, you have some sympathy with the gypsy population you will find yourself in a very small minority. I've only attended one meeting of residents threatened with a few gypsies nearby; it nearly turned into a lynching party.

Keep asking around. Builders and architects may know of properties for sale. Even consider a bigger cottage or a house which could be split up; if there are two plots or two adjacent cottages, try to get a builder to take over the one you don't want. You sometimes find pairs of semi-detached cottages for sale with one tenanted; the price may be tempting but buying property for investment with a tenant in may mean a long, fraught wait for possession, so take great care.

When travelling around, read notices pinned on gates and buildings—they may lead you to people applying for permission to develop, or they may warn you of new motorways. Don't be scared off by Closing or Demolition Orders; you won't be able to live in a place with one of these hanging over it but if you check with the local council (*before* buying, of course) you may find them willing to negotiate. At the very least they will advise you what work needs to be done to lift the Orders.

If there are complications, then buy a place 'subject to such and such'. For instance, our Coxwold cottage was originally a private dwelling converted into a doctor's surgery; we bought it subject to planning permission being given to revert it to a private house. If planning had been refused then the sale would have fallen through.

Finally, search, search, then search again; don't give up. When you have found somewhere which you think is right for you, go back a second time for another look. Go back a third time and if possible a fourth time so that you get over your initial love affair with the place and reality takes over.

2

Unusual or Abroad

Most people would consider that they had enough on their plate renovating a traditional cottage in a traditional setting, yet some take on the greater challenge of something more unusual. If you are part of this brave breed then the National Trust and Forestry Commission occasionally sell off properties. These may not be unusual in form but in setting, being so remote as to have problems over essential services.

If you are prepared to take a gamble on something off-beat then tell estate agents that you will consider anything, and stress *anything*. The main advantage with unusual buildings will often be the positioning; it goes without saying, so I'll say it, that windmills are fairly high up, so that they are near to wind, which could mean good views. Watermills will be near to water, and so on.

Schools increasingly come up for sale as the population declines but they do need care. They are often fine examples of Victorian architecture with tremendous brick detailing—as important to the history of architecture as old railway stations. So, however unwillingly you used to go to school, convert one with care, respect the original and don't try to hide the fact that it *is* a converted school. One snag may be that windows are high up so that you have to stand on a chair to see out.

You could consider lighthouses, oast houses or water towers, while barns are often in nice settings although planning permission for them may be difficult (if not impossible) in many areas and if a barn falls down you will not necessarily be given permission to rebuild it. As with schools, don't attempt to disguise what a barn or other building originally was.

If you are considering an old church or vicarage, apply to the local branch of the church in the area in which you are interested because the head offices are unlikely to have lists. Most of the redundant

Methodist churches have already been sold, by the way. One advantage with churches, chapels and schools is that you can easily find them on your vetting journeys because they will be marked on many maps, they certainly will be on the splendid Ordnance Survey 1:50,000 maps. In general, chapels will be simpler to convert than churches. One problem with an old church may be that it has an adjacent cemetery; you can't just start digging people up, so discuss things with the vendors.

Apply to the local branch of British Rail if you feel you would like to live in an old railway station. You sometimes see ads for old railway carriages (as opposed to buildings) as dwellings; these may have some novelty appeal as holiday cottages but are often difficult to sell and certainly expensive to haul around the country. In addition, it must get tiresome pushing one up and down every time someone wants to use the toilet.

If you have imagination and determination, you can convert almost anything and with unusual places you can afford to be daring and original in your planning if the Authorities will let you. (I notice that my typist as automatically put a capital 'A' for authorities, which perhaps reflects the awe in which we tend to hold them. But they are people aren't they? And they are paid out of *our* taxes!)

If you buy a lofty building, consider if there is room for a gallery area by putting in an additional floor—this should be possible with schools, chapels, and, possibly, with old smithies. Galleries featuring plenty of natural pine can look particularly attractive in such places.

Of course, there may be problems in converting unusual places. There may be things inside which you can't remove easily—for instance, an old mill may have ancient machinery in it (leave it in place and make it a feature, maybe even charge people to come and see it). In addition, planners may rightly insist that the exterior must remain close to the original in appearance, which may mean having special windows and doors purpose built; these will be vastly more expensive than off-the-shelf ones.

If you glance through *Exchange & Mart* in your search for the

Figure 6. *Old schools are usually well built and have a sufficiency of toilets. Windows tend to be very high off the ground.*
Figure 7. *Old barns are often in nice positions but, with settlement problems and general lack of protection against damp, it may be cheaper to pull one down and rebuild rather than renovate. Planning permission may be difficult.*

Figure 8 (Above) *and* Figure 9 (Right). *This fine Cotswold cottage was converted from an old forge. The long portion on the left was the workroom and made a splendid living room with a studio gallery at the end nearest the camera in* Figure 9. *Schools and chapels often have headroom for similar galleries to be added.*

unusual, keep an eye on the 'portable buildings' section because occasionally you will find chalets or prefabs which would make holiday letting units or at least act as temporary accommodation while you perform major surgery on a cottage. However, if you decide to buy something simple, such as a holiday chalet, as a weekend cottage then be sure it complies with the local planning regulations and that there are no restrictions. Some may be leasehold and on very short leases at that. Others may just have a temporary licence and not be for permanent accommodation, so you may not be able to spend Christmas there.

Do beware of leisure plots. I know the onus is always on buyers to beware but the racket of carving up pleasant land, say alongside a river, into tiny squares, then kidding people that they may eventually get planning permission, is the unsavoury side of selling. The onus is also on you to take great care if you decide to buy abroad. Another minefield!

Buying abroad

You are going to be much more vulnerable if buying something abroad

than you would be at home because clearly you won't be so au fait with the legal complications, nor with handling builders. If you consider buying somewhere overseas then do choose a location with a good climate. You can find scenery as beautiful as anywhere in the world in the UK; you can even find nude bathing beaches, which is why I am growing a beard (someone has to fetch the ice-cream). Why go abroad for what you can find at home? Head for the sun instead. However, in searching for the sun, don't automatically plump for the Côte de Gatwick with fish and chips and English spoken everywhere. Try to get a little bit away from the popular tourist places, although if you are considering an overseas property as a letting investment it must be reasonably easy to get to—people will not book a second year if they have to take a ten-mile camel ride to reach your cottage.

Never buy a place abroad without seeing it. *Don't* rely on photographs or even a cine film to give you a feel for the place; go and see for yourself. Talk to people who have lived in an area for some time, not just those in their first flush of enthusiasm for the place. This particularly applies if you plan to live in a place permanently because meeting the same small group of English-speaking people week after week, reminiscing about the supermarket or golf club in Guildford is not everyone's idea of heaven. Just as when searching for property in Britain, draw up a checklist—will you want English-speaking schools, access to shops and so on? If anything, devote even more time to this planning stage for a property abroad than for one at home because the results of getting things wrong will be more disastrous.

If you are thinking of buying abroad, do keep in mind the political situation. One hilarious feature of recent years has been that the professional pundits have regularly failed to forecast the world's most momentous events, so unless you have a much clearer crystal ball you will have difficulty in forecasting just how politically stable a country is going to remain.

Having vetted a place abroad, don't hand over cash to a third party without proper authorisation from the vendor, and be sure you have identified the actual vendor; properties in Spain, for instance, may be owned by whole families and, just when you think you have a deal, mother-in-law may *paso doble* on it (she would). Beware of high sounding guarantees, such as one guaranteeing a high letting rate if you put a place into the hands of a local agent; guarantees are only as good as the companies giving them. If you are buying at an early stage of a large development, it may be many years before building finishes on the site and in the meantime there will be builders' rubble etc around, while if it is an inexpensive development with many plots, you may find difficulty in reselling until after all the sites have been sold. Some developments rely on land deposits and payments for the actual development of the site. If the developers do not have sufficient funds to complete the work without relying on this income, your investment could be lost if the developers cannot complete the scheme because of changes in market conditions etc. So if you are negotiating with a company for an overseas property, ask your bank manager for a status report on them and, if in any doubt, stick to the big agencies, the ones with reputations to lose.

Don't let the promised sunshine dazzle you to the fact that snags may occur with a property abroad. For instance, friends of ours got sent a hefty bill for new roof tiles for their cottage in Spain. On their next visit they could not really tell whether anything had been done or not; they suspected the latter. If you have to go to law over an issue, fighting in a foreign court may not be much fun. I once got involved in a minor traffic accident in Greece and the complications were far worse than if it had happened in Grimsby.

If you decide to go ahead and buy somewhere abroad, don't necessarily expect your local solicitor to cope. You may need to find a big firm with overseas branches and overseas experience; the international branch of your bank may be able to give you some guidance.

Your bank will also be able to advise you on the latest currency rules (if any) but keep in mind that any transactions will be subject to our own and *local* exchange regulations. Incidentally, you may find a bank uneasy or unwilling to accept a foreign property as security for something else (say, a business venture); you can come unstuck with overseas properties if you run into financial problems and have to sell quickly.

Remember, if you buy a cottage abroad in a country with a lower inflation rate than ours then your money may not be keeping pace with inflation as well as it would if invested in this country. Mind, that's a bit simplistic, because you also need to take into account the relative values of currencies, so discuss it with your accountant.

You will have gathered by now that I am not wildly enthusiastic about buying and converting a cottage abroad; timesharing doesn't make my adrenalin flow either for many of the same reasons. You may call me a coward (there's no need to shout) but all I can say is that of our friends who have tried buying abroad, more have had problems than not. But let us turn to the Mother Country and let us suppose that you have found your heavenly haven. What next? Well, you need to vet it before you buy, so let us move on to the following chapter.

3

Vetting

Less than a fifth of people buying a house go to the expense of having a full structural survey. This could be because if you have a survey done, then don't proceed with the purchase, you have wasted your money. So if you are sure that you are interested in buying a particular cottage, sort out with the vendor or his agent that the expected price is within your reach *before* you decide to commission a survey. Don't confuse a valuation with a structural survey. A valuation for a building society could take 20 minutes, a full structural survey a few hours, with a commensurate increase in cost. Building societies (and other sources of finance) are mainly concerned about whether they can get their money back if you default, so a lender's survey is just a valuation for their protection. However, following heavy breathing by the Office of Fair Trading and others, building societies will show you a copy of 'their' survey (so they should—you will be paying for it) while a surveyor approved by a building society should be able to do a full structural survey for you (if you wish) *and* a valuation survey for your building society at the same time. If you select this method, you should agree the fee with the surveyor in advance.

I must confess that I have never had a full-blooded survey done but if you feel you would like the reassurance of one, then you need to look for a member of the Royal Institution of Chartered Surveyors or the Incorporated Society of Valuers and Auctioneers. You may feel that an 'inspection report scheme', which is a sort of half-way house survey, may be adequate for you—the surveyor will give guidance on plumbing and wiring but, for instance, will not take up floorboards to check for rot. Whatever form of survey (if any) you decide to have done, brief a surveyor properly and make sure he confirms in writing the terms and scope of his engagement and, above all, the cost. You won't find specific scale fees quoted for structural surveys as they are left to be arranged according to the circumstances, age, size and

Figure 10 (Left). *Rot on windows tends, predictably, to be at the bottom. Consider if it is possible to splice in new wood before rushing to buy a new window (which may be expensive if it has to be specially made).*

Figure 11 (Below). *The less attractive rear of the cottage shown in* Figure 4. *Walls built out as an extension of a cottage, as here, tend to suck in water.*

condition of the property, so try haggling and obtain more than one quotation. If a survey recommends having drains, electrics and other services specially tested, then there will be further expense. Check what indemnity the surveyor has—it could be some comfort if your roof blows off later—and, by the way, don't use the vendor's estate agents to do a survey; you will save nothing and could incur some risk (no responsible selling agent would do one anyway).

When you receive your surveyor's report, sit down with a strong drink before you read it because it will be so full of gloom and doom that you will immediately abandon all hope. But pause. *Of course* it is going to be a tale of woe if you have asked for a full survey because a surveyor is being paid to point out faults and every cottage has plenty. Ring the surveyor and try to get a realistic view because the real question you want answered is, quite simply, 'Is it worth buying?' Use any horror stories in the survey to haggle for a lower price. If there is something dramatically wrong, the moneylenders may keep back part of the advance until the fault is put right; we had 20 per cent held back on one cottage until the roof was repaired.

All-in-all, it is entirely healthy that consumer power has helped to sweep away some of the unnecessary mystique about formal surveys. As far as most people are concerned, a theodolite could be a guru living in a cave. If you have prodded around several places and have a bit of DIY experience then, provided you are not buying a place for a million pounds, you should be capable of doing your own survey without the expense of a formal one.

Faults in old cottages usually stem from:

- Inadequate or non-existent services
- Inadequate lighting
- General decay or old age (I know the feeling)
- Damp due to broken guttering, roof problems or the lack of a damp-proof course

Set off to do a survey in your old clothes, with a notebook, tape-measure, hammer and screwdriver and start by vetting the outside thoroughly. Ideally, you need to pair of binoculars to study the roof. Take care though—I once got shouted at by a husband who thought I was peering at his wife dressing in a bedroom in the cottage next door. The very idea! Anyone would think I'd never seen a lace-edged petticoat before.

You need not be put off by the odd missing roof tile but check if the ridge itself is fairly straight. If not, the timbers may need replacing and this can be expensive. Usually the ridge is the last thing to go on a roof because, logically, less water rests up there than at the bottom, which is the most vulnerable, so check if there are any dips in the roof line lower down.

Moving down the outside of the house, are the walls bulging? If they are bulging at the top, it could mean that the ceiling joists have gone or span the wrong way, or are tied too high up; whatever the cause, the house is spreading. It can be buttressed but you should certainly run to an expert for advice. Tie rods through a cottage should also have you reaching for expert advice, even if they have got pretty designs on their outside ends instead of the more usual crosses. Such rods mean that at some time the walls have started spreading. The owner of one cottage I viewed was convinced a tie rod was a leaking water pipe because of condensation on the cold metal.

Prod at outside window frames with a screwdriver—if it sinks in, that means they have rot. However, this may not automatically mean new windows because it may be possible to splice in a new piece of wood rather than replace a whole window (we had this done at one cottage and the cost was about a quarter of that for a new window).

When you get inside, jump up and down on the floors—if you go through to the floor below it means there is a weakness in the flooring (I hope your broken leg will soon be better). Tap on the walls to test their solidity; there will be a dull sound if plaster is not firm, although this is not a major tragedy. Ignore torn wallpaper and scruffy wood-work because paint can make a dramatic difference. Ignore damp patches *provided* you can trace the cause and it can be cured easily. Prod with a knife or screwdriver to see if the inside woodwork has any rot but don't necessarily be put off—it is possible to replace rotten timber—although you should seek further advice. Check under carpets and lino for rot or other damage.

Rust round radiator fittings may mean that they need attention, while if one wall is panelled or furnished out of character with the rest of a room it may be hiding a trouble spot. Old cottages often are boarded round the lower half of the downstairs walls—a sure sign of damp. Don't view if you have a heavy cold because you really need a sense of smell to sniff out dry rot and bad drains. If in doubt, a woodworm/dry rot survey is worth while. The fee should be absorbed in the cost of the job if the people who do the survey are given the contract later.

Remember that if you are applying for grants you will almost certainly have to put in a damp-proof course.

Take a torch when searching so that you can clamber about in the loft. Chat to the vendor's children as you go round because they may innocently reveal horrendous problems that the owner would rather you didn't know about. Keep in mind that a vendor should give honest answers to your questions. For instance, if you ask about subsidence and other specific faults and he lies, and you can prove it, you can sue later (obviously it helps if you have a witness with you).

This section on surveying could go on for ever (what do you mean, it's starting to feel like it?) so let me just stress that the more you prod around, the more chance you have of establishing if a place is worth buying. You may not have the expertise to check electrics but the state and age of the sockets and general wiring will give you a clue as to whether you should seek professional advice.

Perhaps the best way of all to survey a cottage (particularly at the lower end of the price range) is first find your builder then persuade him to vet the cottage with you. He will have a balanced view of things if he is used to working on similar properties in the area. Something that frightens you may be dismissed by the builder with a shrug; conversely, something you have missed may be pointed out by him as a very expensive fault.

4

Buying

This chapter assumes that you have found the place you want, you have vetted it, and you are now ready to go through the legal process of actually buying it. Having reached this stage, do be decisive. Take the plunge. If you spend weeks agonising or haggling over £50 or ½ per cent on interest charges while prices are escalating, then you will have slipped back on the property ladder. Provided you buy in a sensible area and don't go mad, it really is difficult to lose on property. This assumes you have gone through a long sifting process and are not buying while still starry eyed over somewhere and note that I said *provided you buy in a sensible area*. If you buy a cottage in a district that is rapidly becoming run-down, perhaps through wholesale factory closures, then of course you can lose money, but in general if you pick somewhere sound and simple in a reasonable area, then your money will be safe. As I said earlier, the crazy boom years of rapidly escalating property prices may have gone but, long term, a sensibly bought and renovated cottage should not be a bad investment.

Legal advice

If you are ready to buy, you need a solicitor. There is an air of mystery and magic about the legal profession which I suspect they encourage at times (it helps to keep up their fees). It seems absurd that I can sell you a Rolls-Royce in ten seconds (it's only had one careful owner, squire) yet it takes weeks to sell you a house at half the price, but that is the law. The Swansea Vehicle Licensing Computer, despite all the brickbats hurled at it, works well considering the complexities; there should be a similar system for property.

Solicitors will be reluctant to admit it but much of the work in their offices is done by clerks, so you may consider you have equal abilities and therefore could do your own soliciting. Well, if you feel this way, there are several books on the subject; I enjoyed *The Conveyancing Fraud* written by a solicitor, Michael Joseph, which lifts the lid off the business and struck me as a thoroughly entertaining read. But, and it is a huge 'but', the conveyancing of a house is not as simple as painting the skirting boards, and an old cottage could present more complicated legal problems than the purchase of a modern house. In addition, the professional Brotherhood may gang up on you and the vendor's solicitors and your own moneylenders may push you towards using a solicitor. To me it is such a tricky area that I'd rather put my energies into developing the property itself, using experts to do the actual conveyancing. So I use solicitors. They are all covered by professional negligence insurance and by the Law Society's Compensation Fund and really, apart from the fact that they take over a fairly complicated job for you, the main advantage in using a solicitor is the simple peace of mind you get from having purchased through a professional. In one of my numerous transactions, my solicitor saved me from one major clanger, for which I will be eternally grateful. He spotted something which I am quite sure I would have missed had I been doing my own conveyancing.

But, horses for courses. If a friend boasts that a sharp solicitor got him off a drink/driving charge (do you really need friends like that?) that solicitor may not necessarily be right for a complicated house transaction. The best way to find a solicitor is via a friend, *not* an estate agent, nor for that matter via a bank manager (the 'you scratch my back' system may apply). Happily, I count my solicitors as friends and if you do enough work with yours, you may get into the same fortunate position. If you have no particular solicitor in mind and you are about to embark on a one-off transaction, phone round a few solicitors and ask for a rough quote for doing the work. You may get a haughty brush-off from one or two of them, but so what? The legal system is part of our glorious heritage, as are the stocks and the Bloody Tower; some pompous members of the legal profession should be put in both.

The solicitor you choose should be on your building society's approved list so that he can act for you *and* the society to help cut costs. (I keep referring to 'building society' when I really mean the organisation lending you the money. It's not sloppy writing, it's just that 'moneylenders' smacks of pawnbrokers and I hope you aren't *that* desperate for a cottage.) When you contact a solicitor, be armed with every possible piece of information. Have the name and address of the seller, the address of the property, whether it is leasehold or freehold (more likely the latter), the price you have agreed and, if possible, the name of the seller's agents and solicitor. Brief your solicitor if you have sorted out with the vendor any particular arrangement over carpets, or whether there is an open issue over planning permission. Let him know when you are hoping for completion. This can take weeks, although it should be possible within a month provided you are not a petal in a long daisy-chain of people stacked up buying from each other. Sign *nothing* without advice! You will need to be particularly brisk in your approach if gazumping is going on; this can still happen for a particularly desirable snip even if the general property market is in a slump. Arguably, if two people are being forced into a contract race, the owner of the property should agree to pay the expenses of the loser; however, although there are mutterings from time to time about legislation against gazumping (it's such a splendid word it would almost be a pity if it fell into disuse) being realistic this is unlikely to happen.

Making an offer

Having contacted a solicitor, the next stage in the buying process is to make an offer 'subject to contract', and perhaps 'subject to survey' and perhaps 'subject to such-and-such on planning permission'. It is usual to pay a token deposit of £50 or so; you may be asked for up to 10 per cent by an estate agent but if so, refuse. You don't have to pay that amount at this stage of the proceedings. In fact, the deposit you are paying the estate agent is really meaningless because if you pull out or get gazumped and the vendor sells to someone else, you will get your money back; the deposit puts no obligation on either of you. Your token deposit should go into a clients' account at the estate agent's bank. What happens to the interest on it? Don't ask. Incidentally, don't pay a deposit directly to the seller in person; it should go through a solicitor and receipts should be obtained for any money handed over.

At this stage, if you are married, consider entering into the purchase under joint ownership. It means no extra work for anyone. You and your spouse both have to sign the contracts and, if the Transfer is appropriately worded, it means that the property passes automatically to the survivor in case of death without a will having to be proved. It also has advantages for Inheritance Tax. Mind you, joint ownership assumes you think your marriage will survive the rigours of renovating. Perhaps a dangerous assumption.

Before we get too far into this chapter, I had better make it clear that things are different in Scotland for buying and selling houses.

Solicitors buy and sell as well as estate agents and there are many other differences. I've never bought or sold in Scotland—it's too far away for me for a holiday home—so I have no practical experience; the *Which?* book on buying and selling houses has an excellent chapter on the system. A friend recently bought a cottage on the banks of Loch Ness with no problems and Scotland is one place where you can still find but-and-bens (small cottages) at low prices *but* the prices are low because demand is too, and the cost of travelling there can be frightening for Sassenachs.

Contracts

Moving back south of the border, down Mablethorpe way, once you have expressed an interest in buying, and made an offer 'subject to contract', your solicitor should get a draft contract from the vendor's solicitor. In return he will send an Enquiries Before Contract form. This is a standard document which asks questions about boundaries, any guarantees on the property, what defects have become apparent, whether any adverse claims have been made by other parties, what is the rateable value, what fixtures and fittings are included, what services are connected, and so on. There is a space on the form for the vendor's solicitor to reply. If a reply is too vague—such as 'we believe so' to an important question—then ask your solicitor to pursue the matter further. Strangely, the replies (and I quote) 'are believed to be correct, but the accuracy is not guaranteed', in other words it is not safe to continue without the enquiries! Therefore your solicitor will send two forms to local authorities. One is an Enquiries of District Councils form which is concerned with finding out things like: is the property properly drained into a sewer, are there any resolutions affecting the property under the Public Health Act, has the council started any proceedings in respect of infringement of building regulations? The other form goes under the splendid title of 'Register of Local Land Charges, Requisition for Search and Official Certificate of Search'. Quite simply all this does is establish if there are things called 'local land charges' on the property. For instance, it will discover if there are any grants to be repaid or any planning permission with conditions attached. These forms look very official and impressive but they really don't reveal all that much. Because of the volume of work, councils send *printed* answers to many of the questions and often there will be bland replies to others; this may all be reasonable enough if they are dealing with an estate of identical new houses—you may need to check answers with care for a more unusual property.

GENERAL ENQUIRIES	REPLIES
	These replies are given on behalf of the proposed Vendor and without responsibility on the part of his solicitors their partners or employees. They are believed to be correct but the accuracy is not guaranteed and they do not obviate the need to make appropriate searches, enquiries and inspections.
1. Boundaries	
(A) To whom do all the boundary walls, fences, hedges and ditches belong?	1(a) The left-hand and rear boundaries are thought to belong to the property.
(B) If no definite indications exist, which has the Vendor maintained or regarded as his responsibility?	
2. Disputes	2. No.
Is the Vendor aware of any past or current disputes regarding boundaries, easements, covenants or other matters relating to the property or its use?	
3. Notices	3. None to the Vendor's knowledge but the property is sold subject to any there might be.
Please give particulars of all notices relating to the property, or to matters likely to affect its use or enjoyment, that the Vendor (or to his knowledge, any predecessor in title) has given or received	

Figure 12. *An extract from an Enquiries Before Contract form showing the rather vague replies. It is up to you, through your solicitor, to pursue any doubtful points.*

As well as the work your solicitor is doing in establishing whether there is any charge for roads, any planning problems, any potential motorways, any fence repairs, any boundary disputes . . . as well as all that, you should be doing your own checking. For instance, is there car parking space? You don't have a divine right to park on the piece of road outside your front door—if your car obstructs the highway then you are breaking the law.

Keep in mind that a solicitor will not necessarily visit the cottage you are buying although he should if there is anything unusual about the purchase. You and your solicitor should be checking things like the rights of way for drainage over neighbouring land. In particular, beware of developments—are airports or new motorways planned. Call to see the planning officer and find out. Don't expect a search to throw up what is likely to happen to the orchard next door—so sniff around, talk to planners, and if you find out anything then alert your solicitor because oral replies carry no weight; any queries must be followed through in writing.

Access

Do make sure that proper access to the cottage is established. You should be able to enjoy the legal rights to use the necessary means of access to your property but there can be squabbles such as over access to the rear of terraced cottages and, if they arise, they can be difficult ones. Anyway, in the fullness of time (and the time may be fuller than you had hoped) the various forms come back. You may get other correspondence with the return of your search form, like this for one of your cottages:

> In returning to you the completed Official Certificate of Search, together with Replies to Enquiries, I have been asked to draw your attention to the fact that this property is within an area listed as being of archaeological significance.
>
> Should any works be carried out that would substantially disturb the sub-soil, you should notify the County Planner to enable him to arrange for an approved archaeologist to inspect the works and record any archaeological features which might appear.

We didn't find anything apart from some ancient lemonade bottles.

At this stage you may have to start negotiating over various points, for instance for one cottage we faced clauses stating that if we sold within a given time, the vendor could buy back from us:

(a) The vendor will retain an option to re-purchase the properties if they are re-offered for sale, either at the first sale or subsequent sales, within ten years, which even is the longer time.

(b) The price will then be the current value for the improved properties and an arbitration clause is to be contained in the contract. The right will be subject to a minimum price, plus the cost of all improvements when ever carried out and all repairs during the first year, less any grants.

As we were buying from a farmer, it seemed entirely reasonable that he should have first refusal if we sold although we modified clause (b) to read 'less any grants which have to be repaid'.

You may get restrictive covenants stopping you from doing certain things but don't lose too much sleep over them because they may have been imposed by someone long since dead or for reasons now totally irrelevant. If somebody in 1906 stipulated that such-and-such should happen, you can probably forget all about it now. Once we had to agree that: 'The vendor reserves the right to approve alterations to the exterior of the properties, the approval not to be unreasonably withheld.' I too was anxious to preserve the look of the place and was happy with this condition. Later in our renovation I sent a very simple sketch of our ideas to the vendor and there was no problem in getting agreement. I guess the vendor was anxious to stop anyone adding Georgian windows and a massive front door with bullseye glass panels to the tiny cottage. Don't laugh, it's often done.

Irrespective of any conditions imposed by the vendor, you will be wise to clear any major planning problems, such as making a change of use, before completing a purchase. If you are buying a barn, then buy it 'subject to planning permission for conversion into a dwelling' because it won't be much use to you without such permission. However, if you are planning only minor changes, it is unreasonable to expect a vendor to wait a long time while you struggle to get planning permission, and he may well not do so if the property market is booming.

During the negotiating stages, establish what fittings, cupboards and so on will be left in the cottage and put this in writing. You buy the house in the condition it was in on the day contracts were exchanged. Some mean devils even take bulbs away with them (both lighting and plant) while the cost of curtain tracking can mount up if it has all been taken away. Any solicitor worth his salt will insist that the contract contains a full list of any items included in the price, such as storage heaters, wall lights and so on.

When all the searches have been completed and both you and your solicitor (and the vendor and his solicitor) are happy and a form of contract has been agreed, copies are sent to all parties. At this stage your solicitor should send you copies of the searches together with explanations of unusual points. You may think that he is doing this to keep you in the picture; he is, but he is also doing it to pass the buck. If he points out that something cannot be established, that means he won't accept responsibility if there is a problem over it later.

Once everyone is happy with the form of contracts, they are exchanged. This is a key part of the conveyancing process. You will be asked to pay 10 per cent deposit and you are committed to buying the cottage, subject to the seller proving that he has the right to sell it. At this point the vendor is still responsible for the maintenance of the property but the purchaser becomes responsible for its insurance. If you are on a tight time schedule with your renovation, you may want to get possession of a property after the exchange of contracts but before the final completion, either to carry out repairs and decoration or even to take up residence. It *may* be possible to organise this via a licence arranged between both parties' solicitors, with you paying a suitable rate of interest on the balance of the outstanding money (instead of a rental) until legal completion takes place. You may simply want to go in to strip off wallpaper and the vendor may readily give you access for this (I was given permission the three times I asked). You are less likely to get permission to start knocking down walls because if you then become bankrupt or die, the vendor may be left with an even more derelict property. When you exchange contracts, your solicitor will get the vendor's contract signed by him, together with an 'abstract of title'. This is a summary of all the relevant portions of deeds which trace the vendor's title; in other words, it proves he has a right to sell the cottage.

Having received the abstract of title, your solicitor has 14 days to investigate the title and then submit a draft Conveyance or Transfer to the vendor's solicitor. He will make main searches against some former owners and the vendors which, for instance, will establish if any second mortgage has not been paid off (this will be registered as a charge against the property at the Land Registry).

Incidentally, if you had planned to do your own conveyancing, hasn't all this rigmarole convinced you that you would be better spending your time planning the actual renovation?

If for any reason you start to drag your feet, or for that matter the vendor's solicitors are inefficient, either party can serve a 'notice to complete' if the completion date has passed without any action; if the notice is not complied with, it is then a case of going to court for an order. However, if all goes well, completion will take place one month from the exchange of contracts. At the completion ceremony (and one almost expects a military band to play while a flag is raised) solicitors meet, the purchase money is handed over, usually in the form of a banker's draft, and your solicitor will get the deeds for the property, which of course will go to the people who have lent you the money. The cottage is now yours.

I hope you will both be very happy.

But, caution—are you quite sure you bought the place with vacant possession? If you get a hint that the vendor is selling because of marital problems and a divorce is pending, then it is a wise move for you or your solicitor to check that the place is actually empty before you finally complete; you may not be too pleased if you find an extra wife comes as part of your fixtures and fittings. Oh, I don't know though.

The final thing to sort out is the handing over of the keys, which should be done at the same time as completion; quite often keys will be left with the estate agent who dealt with you in the first place.

It only remains to notify the local council of the change of ownership. You will normally have agreed to pay an apportionment of the rates, and if you are changing the use of the place then you will need to get the valuation list altered; usually just a case of writing to the council. An empty property is not usually subject to rates for a few months—check the local position because some authorities may levy rates the moment a stick of furniture goes in. I was surprised to find that the rateable value of our Yorkshire cottage went *down* when it reverted to a dwelling from a doctors' surgery. I would have thought doctors more essential than second home owners in a rural area to help hold a community together. Ours not to reason why.

When budgeting, keep in mind that the rateable value of your cottage will increase if you make major improvements to it.

The reckoning

You have one other little treat in store—your solicitor's bill. A solicitor is entitled to charge 'a fair and reasonable amount'. If they are being honest, solicitors will admit that a typical conveyance involves around eight hours' work if you are buying, seven if you are selling. In theory, there is no more work for a solicitor in dealing with an expensive house than a cheap one, yet the bill may be higher, perhaps because of increased responsibility, more likely because it is what the market will bear. Note that you will be faced with VAT on solicitors' fees and you will also have to pay any relevant Stamp Duty and maybe Land Registry fees as well. These change from time to time so ask your solicitor for the dreaded details before you do your budgeting.

Caution: you may be charged 'chatting time' by your solicitor, so if you prolong an interview while you show him slides of your holiday in Majorca, then you may pay for the privilege (in my view everyone should have to pay to show holiday slides). Although 'recommended charges' are announced from time to time—but not in a very loud voice—by the Law Society in consultation with the Building Societies Association, the Law Society does not encourage solicitors to break down their invoices too much, which is why you will find reference to 'voluminous correspondence' and so on, without much specific detail. If you are unhappy with your solicitor's invoice—and a survey showed 60 per cent of people think they charge too much, so you will not be alone—you can dispute it or at the very least ask for a breakdown. If you are still not happy with the explanation, you have 30 days to apply to the Law Society for the bill to be checked but suing solicitors is not easy—they are the experts. Best of all, obtain a quotation in advance covering estimated fees, Stamp Duty etc.

Tenders and auctions

All this has assumed that you have the money to pay for the transaction. Before we cover the sordid subject of money in more detail, let us briefly consider buying a cottage via tenders and auctions. A tender has to be submitted sealed, and all tenders submitted are opened on a particular day and the tenders are binding on those who make them. If you put in your tender 'I'll bid a penny more than anyone else' it is unlikely to be accepted because it could easily make the whole sale a shambles. A vendor does not have to accept the highest, or any, tender; for instance if he thinks you want to turn his humble cottage into a holiday camp then he could turn you down for that reason.

I dislike the tender system. Auctions are much to be preferred because they are more open affairs. At an auction the bid of the individual can clinch the sale so if you are nodding off at the time the hammer falls, you've bought it. You will be asked to sign a binding contract and pay 10 per cent deposit. Note that word *binding*. You can't back out so don't treat an auction frivolously. It is vitally important that you don't bid without first carrying out at least the basic checks that would normally take place prior to contract in a conventional purchase. So make sure that your solicitor has obtained a clear local authority search and satisfactory replies to the usual pre-contract enquiries before you trip off to an auction.

You will sometimes see cottages offered 'for sale by private treaty or by auction later'. This may be a vendor's attempt to put pressure on buyers to agree a sale quickly or it may be that they don't want to be tied down on price but prefer to sound out the market.

Auctions are usually conducted by professionals but they can still fall flat. I attended an auction to buy our Yorkshire cottage and just as the auctioneer was about to begin, someone in the audience stood up and said that he was acting on behalf of a potential purchaser. He stated that he had checked with the National Park that morning and there was some query over whether a change of use would be agreed from a surgery back to a private dwelling. The atmosphere in the auction room became gloomy and the cottage dismally failed to reach the reserve. I got my solicitor to check and he found there was nothing to prevent the change of use back to a dwelling, so I phoned the estate agents and bought via a miniature phone auction of my own (I suspect with the vendor standing alongside the agent).

Don't get carried away if you attend an auction. Be quite positive before you go that the cottage is what you want and be firm about what you are prepared to bid up to. You may find that the bids you are competing against are actually being 'pulled off the wall' by the auctioneer just to jolly the sale along. If a condition of sale at an auction says that the property is offered 'subject to reserved right to bid', the bloke enthusiastically bidding against you may be the vendor, which explains his enthusiasm. Care.

5

Money Matters

The key thing to do when you set out on a financial pilgrimage to raise funds for your cottage is to *budget carefully and realistically*. Do list *all* the things you are likely to have to pay for. You may have to budget for some or all of the following:

- Purchase of property
- Legal costs:
  Solicitors' costs
  Land Registry Fees
  Stamp Duty
- Bridging loan finance
- Cost of renovation and VAT
- Mortgage repayments even if you are not yet able to live in the cottage
- Mortgage arrangement fees
- Deposits for gas and electricity boards.

Be *pessimistic* because it is certain that contingencies will crop up and you need to be prepared for them. If you decide to live in a caravan on the site while your cottage is renovated and you use the builder's labourers for an hour or two to manhandle it into position, who is going to pay? Certainly not the builder if he has any sense; it will be charged to you, so budget for it. If you spend a lot of time driving to and from the cottage, then your petrol bills could amount to a sizeable sum. Again, allow for this in your budget.

If you plan to use the cottage for holiday letting then I suggest that you need an accountant, preferably a lively one. Remember that tax *avoidance* is not a crime (though *evasion* is) so don't feel any shame about it; the government grab enough in taxes and it is only sensible to avoid paying unnecessarily. Small things mount up—for instance I've used a room in my house as an office to write this book, so it will appear on my tax return. If you have never used an accountant, a bright one should be able to save the cost of his fees in the first year and if you are letting your cottage as a business you can charge accountancy fees against tax. Like solicitors, accountants charge by the time spent on your affairs so use their time wisely, which means briefing them properly.

But assuming that you have taken financial advice and have drawn up a rough budget, now you have to find the money. Some people may have what is called 'mattress money' or 'deed box banking'—cash which has not been declared to the taxman. If they are buying a £25,000 cottage and pay £5,000 'off the book' and £20,000 'on' (handing over £5,000 in cash) this helps them to 'launder' the money and make it more legitimate. If it is not their 'principal private residence' then they will have to pay increased Capital Gains Tax, of course, if they sell the property, unless they do the same thing again (or die). All very complicated and let me stress that I am *not* condoning such tax evasion—just pointing out that it sometimes happens. Even if your money is 'clean' you may still get a better deal if you pay cash because the person selling may be able to evade some Capital Gains Tax. If nothing else, having cash will demonstrate that you are not caught up in a time-consuming chain.

It may be that you have cash which has been obtained legally, just sitting in your bank. If so, consult your accountant because he (or she, of course) may still advise you (for tax reasons) to borrow the maximum you can, using the cottage as security. The advantages of this are:

(a) It leaves you with cash in case you go over budget on the renovation;
(b) Repayments on a mortgage are fixed in 'old money' which with inflation loses its value, while repayments are made in 'new money';
(c) It improves your 'gearing ratio' if you plan to do another project, eg buy a further cottage for holiday letting.

When my bank manager heard I was writing this book (to some extent he has a vested interest because it will reduce my overdraft) he suggested that a prospective cottage buyer makes financial enquiries for money in the following sequence: (1) bank manager; (2) building society; (3) solicitor; (4) mortgage broker; (5) finance house. I agree with his running order but the money market is so competitive—one could describe it as a jungle—that you should shop around to get the best deal. However, wherever you get the funds, do keep your bank manager in the picture about your plans and tell the truth because managers do not like surprises. I am assuming that you have a bank account, of course—you will certainly need one because people will be chary of dealing with you if they cannot apply for a bank reference. If you are proposing to use a cottage for letting it may be worthwhile at this stage considering a separate bank account, through which all your property activities are channelled.

Incidentally, present your case neatly when writing about loans—which means *typing* letters, not scribbling them on blue-lined paper.

Like solicitors and lawyers, money men may seem a little off-putting for the layman but consider for a moment; bakers sell bread, butchers sell meat, bankers sell money, so don't tremble at going to discuss your proposals with them.

I got a call late one night at home from a bank official when I'd written a long screed asking for help with one cottage. When my heart stopped pounding, I realised that he was actually phoning to offer additional help! This was perhaps unusual because bankers tend to be devout nine to five men but it illustrates that it pays to keep your bank properly briefed.

While money is freely available, you may be able to get 100 per cent of the funds you need (or close to it) for a cottage and your problems will be nearly over (apart from repaying the cash, of course). The percentage loaned may be less for more expensive properties or for what are regarded as 'unconventional' designs. If the loan you need comes within your bank manager's 'discretionary powers' you should be able to get a rapid decision. Bank managers and their branches are graded with lending limits and if your request is over your manager's limit then he has to submit a report to his superiors. It could be quicker to go to a bigger branch but, of course, they will not necessarily know you. It can be a good idea to plan your bank manager well in advance!

If you fail to get what you need at a competitive rate from your bank, your most likely source of funds will be a building society. It may help if you have been an investor with a particular building society but do check a society's policy before depositing your money with them. It is no use investing with a society if you find when you come to buy a cottage that it is totally against their policy to lend on the sort of property you have in mind. Some building societies will not lend on places built before a certain year, others are uneasy about thatched cottages and a few fight shy of Listed Buildings, fearing that the various restrictions on them may make such properties difficult to sell. It may help if your solicitor has good connections with a building society and it certainly makes sense to call in at their local office to chat about their general policy and your plans in particular, bearing in mind that building societies are not in business to help property speculators. Most societies will grant loans on properties needing restoration but will probably make it a condition of a loan that the work is completed within a certain period and they may hold back some of the loan until it is. They may add other clauses, for instance we had one insisting that we carried out woodworm treatment within three months of occupying a cottage.

When applying to a building society for a mortgage, proof of steady employment helps, which is why authors are unpopular. Copies of Form P60 will be requested by the society or they will ask for authority to write to your employer who, if you are on good terms with him, may be optimistic about bonuses or your promotion chances. If you are self-employed, the building society will want to see your books and your tax returns (going back two or three years) so if you have been, shall we say 'pessimistic' in your figures for the taxman, this could rebound on you. A building society will normally ask for a letter from accountants or copies of assessments. Like employers, some co-operative accountants have been known to be rather optimistic about their clients' prospects. It has been known for self-employed people to declare a totally false job with a friend's company; when the building society applies to the friend he co-operates by declaring an income. All very tortuous and either illegal, immoral or fattening but the society is unlikely to bother too much provided repayments are kept up. If a building society lends 2½ times income for people in regular employment, it may only lend 2 times to the self-employed. But shop around because different societies have different policies.

Let me stress that a woman should be able to raise finance as easily (or with the same difficulty) as a man. If not, she should raise hell because most businesses are so nervous of getting bad publicity over sex discrimination that women who persist may get even better treatment than men. I guess the same applies to ethnic minorities.

The married should be able to take both partners' incomes into account when getting a mortgage. Some societies offer 2½ times the annual income of the man, plus once the wife's income, other societies lend up to 3 times the joint income. Most societies will be happier if the wife is over 40 and any kids are at school. You can't blame building societies for being cautious over wives' incomes when you consider the desperately high divorce rate. I'm not sure what calculations are made if you are a polygamist but you deserve sympathetic treatment in view of all the in-laws you will accumulate. Common law wives may be treated as single persons so if yours is jointly buying a cottage with you, both incomes should be taken into account, as in the case of engaged couples before marriage. Moneylenders are, or should be, guardians of money not morals. Normally a society will advance 80 per cent of the purchase price or valuation whichever is the *lower*. Advances in excess of this will be considered if you can offer additional security, or take out a guarantee by an insurance company (for which a single premium charge will be made), or offer the deeds of other property or a government security or a life insurance policy with a surrender value or . . . well, anything which will reassure them that their loan is safe.

A mortgage is different from most other contracts because the rate of interest can vary (sometimes alarmingly); the mortgage deed will specify the period of notice that will need to be given before the society can change the rate. The majority of house buyers repay their mortgages by the annuity method, that is by regular monthly payments, so that over the life of a mortgage—usually 20 or 25 years—the debt, together with the interest, is paid off. If you have an annuity mortgage you should consider taking out a mortgage protection policy for the sake of your family. A 40-year-old man would pay around £4 a month for a policy with an initial sum assured of £10,000 and the mortgage is paid off if he dies. There are mortgage protection policies available which guarantee mortgage cover throughout the term of the loan regardless of how mortgage rates move; it is worth getting this type even though they cost a little more.

As an alternative, you may choose to link a mortgage to an endowment insurance plan under which you only pay interest to the building society, stimultaneously paying a monthly premium to an insurance company. When the mortgage period ends, the proceeds of the insurance policy are used to pay off the building society loan. There are different types of endowment mortgages—I won't bore you with the details because the best for you will depend on your circumstances, so go to your bank manager, solicitor or accountant for advice. Keep in mind, of course, that they will be on commission (around 2 per cent of your annual premium times the number of years the policy is in force) so it is up to you to make the final decision. And a further word of warning—the insurance world sells hard, very hard. Be wary if a change of job gets you a mention in a local or trade paper because you are likely to get charming callers phoning to congratulate you; five minutes into their conversation it will become clear that they are flogging insurance. Glowing pictures may be painted by insurance salesmen of how in 20 years a with-profits endowment policy will not

only pay off a building society loan but will give you at least as much
again to spend. Big deal. Until you consider the effects of inflation. So
. . . don't be too seduced by promises of jam tomorrow, and do check
the performance charts to see which life assurance companies really
do consistently well before taking out a policy.

One *advantage* with an endowment mortgage is that if you die the
loan is paid off in full, not that it will do you much good where you are
going. A *disadvantage* is that if mortgage rates escalate, it is impossible to extend the period of a loan—the higher repayments have to be
met in full.

If you despair of getting a mortgage, you may be tempted by the
glowing advertisements of mortgage brokers. I have never used one
but comments from friends who have suggest that although some
brokers are excellent, one should tread with care because they can sell
hard and they know how to charge. Mortgage brokers may be closely
linked with the insurance world and you could be sold something
extremely profitable in commission to the broker, but less sensible for
you.

Insurance companies may be a good bet for a loan if you are considering an expensive cottage; they may lend more than other sources
although their rates will tend to be higher. If you have an existing
insurance policy, you will probably find that you can borrow at a
reduced rate of interest against the 'surrender value' of the policy.
Normally there will be no value for the first two years but thereafter
there will be. If you have a ten-year-old policy you will probably find
that the surrender value is 80 per cent of the premiums paid to date.
You can borrow 80 per cent of this sum for the rest of the term of the
policy. Such borrowings are often used to pay for children's weddings
but you could possibly use one for a second home.

Other people to approach for loans are the finance houses. If possible get independent advice and if in doubt stick with long-
established, reputable companies. I did and have now bought five
cottages this way with almost no hassle. One advantage with a finance
house is that you will probably get a loan with a fixed monthly repayment, where only the term varies. In other words, if interest rates stay
low your loan will be paid off earlier.

If you are turned down by banks, building societies, insurance companies and finance houses, and busking and raiding your children's
piggy banks fail to raise the funds you need, you may need to consider
even more offbeat sources of finance before heading for a building
society. For instance, some vendors let purchasers pay off part or all
of the purchase price over a period, although if you are offered a deal

like this probe why it is available—it may be the only way to get rid of a place with hidden problems. Your solicitor may have access to trust funds; not common but you can occasionally get a private mortgage this way. You may have wealthy relatives or friends who will lend you the money. I have never been so fortunate but if you are, put everything in writing, otherwise friendships will be damaged; people die or get divorced and loose arrangements can lead to aggravation. Your employers may offer you a private finance deal. Many major organisations now offer this 'perk' and, if interest rates are high, a company loan at 3 or 4 per cent does have very real appeal. Most firms give you a reasonable time after you leave to change a loan and most building societies will take them over but at 1 or 2 per cent over normal rates; in certain industries, eg banking and insurance, a new employer will take over such a loan. Do check the rule on what will happen if you leave before taking a company loan; personally I would hate to be so closely tied to an employer. It may suit the Japanese with their company songs and communal exercises; for we British I think it's jolly unhealthy, old chap.

A local authority could be worth approaching over an oddball property; they could be the best bet if you are a first-time buyer or are planning to divide up a large cottage to make more than one living unit. However, like the building societies, they will not lend money just for the luxury of a second home (mind you, people have been known to lie when making applications) and if there is a financial squeeze they tend to run out of cash early. Anyway, try them; it has been known for local authorities to drop clangers on interest rates and you could get a surprisingly good or depressingly bad deal, depending how they have done their sums.

Having found the money to buy your cottage, you may need more later for improvements although ideally you should budget for it all at once. If you do need more, first approach the people who made your original loan; for instance building societies may give you a home improvement loan which will really consist of topping up your existing mortgage. Incidentally, don't hesitate to bargain between banks if you are not getting much help from yours (although I'm not quite sure what bargaining strength you have in threatening to take your overdraft elsewhere).

If all else fails, you may be able to obtain a finance company's home improvement loan—you will often see advertisements for them in the press. It may be easier to get one than a building society or bank loan, though considerably more expensive because finance houses tend to be lending on more 'suspect' cases and they cover that risk with higher

interest rates. Government regulations from time to time may stipulate that you can only borrow, say 90 per cent of the money you
need.

Having secured a loan for the purchase of a cottage and its renovation, do be sure to get full income tax relief on it. You can't get tax
relief on a loan for a second home but you are allowed to select which
is your principal private residence; it makes sense to declare the most
expensive one *provided* the facts match your story—if you have a flat
in London and a palace in Yorkshire, but work only in London, you will
have difficulty in getting the Yorkshire home treated as a principal
residence. You will get tax relief on any money you borrow to carry out
permanent renovation, eg structural changes, but you won't get tax
relief on money borrowed just to paint the place. The law says
'purchase improving or developing land incuding buildings'. The test
is whether the work you carry out improves the property or merely
puts it back to the state it was in before it began to deteriorate.

Grants

So far, this chapter has been mainly about money flowing out to repay
loans. Now for the good news—you may be eligible for a grant towards
the renovation. Honest. Do you pay tax as a law-abiding citizen? Do
you buy tobacco, spirits, petrol and the countless other things bearing
tax? Then you contribute your share towards the country's revenue, so
don't (as some people foolishly do) feel guilty about applying for
grants. They are available to cover a wide range of work which may be
needed to improve the standard of a cottage or keep one in good
repair. You may have no proper bathroom or no hot and cold water
supply, no inside toilet nor even a kitchen sink. You may need to add a
damp-proof course, or the cottage may have poor lighting or ventilation. All these things can be covered under appropriate grants.
There are several types of house renovation grant available through
local councils; the two most likely to affect you are 'improvement' and
'intermediate' grants. Even before you have completed the purchase
of your cottage, you should do two things: (a) get hold of a copy of the
DOE booklet *Home Improvement Grants* (available from your local
council) and (b) consult the home improvements officer of your council
to get pointed in the right direction. If you are thinking of applying for
a grant do *not* start the work before you are given formal permission,
otherwise you won't get the cash!

Improvement grants are intended to help improve homes to a good
standard; they are not intended to help with improvements to modern

houses or fully equipped houses in good repair, or to enlarge a house to provide more bedroom space, and you will not get a grant for the installation of central heating unless it forms part of a major scheme of improvement. These grants are discretionary, so it is for your local council to decide whether or not to give you one. Their approach may depend on their current budget position; when funds are tight authorities have even been known to haggle over colour schemes.

Cottages improved with the help of improvement grants will usually be expected to reach the following standards after conversion:

- Be likely to have a useful life of at least 30 years.
- Be in reasonable repair.
- Have all the standard amenities (bath, basins etc).
- Meet the following requirements:
  (a) Be substantially free from damp.
  (b) Have adequate natural lighting and ventilation in each habitable room.
  (c) Have adequate and safe provision throughout for artificial lighting and have sufficient and safe electric sockets.
  (d) Be provided with adequate drainage facilities.
  (e) Be in a stable structural condition.
  (f) Have a satisfactory internal arrangement.
  (g) Have satisfactory facilities for preparing and cooking food.
  (h) Be provided with adequate heating.
  (i) Have proper provision for the storage of fuel (where necessary) and for the storage of refuse.
  (j) Have adequate thermal insulation in the roof-space.

Intermediate grants are to help meet the cost of improving homes by putting in missing standard amenities—bath, basins, WCs, hot and cold water. They can also cover works of repair and replacement carried out at the same time, but if the provision of a standard amenity involves extra work (such as an addition to provide a bathroom or a septic tank for a toilet) it may be better to apply for an improvement grant instead of an intermediate grant. Intermediate grants are mandatory so your council *must* give you one if they are satisfied that you meet the basic requirements which apply to all grants. You have a right to a grant even if you do not wish to put in all the standard amenities—and you can get another grant later if you want to put in more. So, for example, if you just want to put in an inside toilet, you can normally get a grant for that without having to carry out any other work at the same time. The council has the right to insist that, once the

work is completed, the house or flat should be fit for human habitation, but if they think it reasonable to do so they may give you a grant
even if the house or flat will still be technically 'unfit'. If an authority is
short of cash it may adopt a tough line on grants—such as by imposing
onerous conditions for a place to count as 'fit for human habitation'.
And there's the rub with grants—you may have to do more work than
you wish. If you run up against a difficult council the fact that your
cottage has had people playing happy families in it for centuries may
not stop officials insisting on larger windows and so on. However, in
certain circumstances the council may agree to reduce or dispense
with some of the conditions.

Grant officers are usually from the Environmental Services
Department—or some equally self-important sounding name—and
do seem to get bogged down in minimum criteria. There is a case for
grants being managed by planning departments whose people are
more likely to have a 'feel' for older places and be more positive in
helping to preserve them.

Incidentally, for cottages in which a registered disabled person is or
will be living, a grant may cover the provision of alternative standard
amenities where existing ones are unsuitable.

If you run into problems as your renovation progresses—you will—
your council may (subject to certain limitations) increase the grant to
cover the additional work if it could not have been reasonably fore-
seen when you made the application. So it pays to stay on good terms
with the officials in case you want to go back cap-in-hand.

Applications for grants have to be made to the council on a pre-
scribed form, together with adequate plans, specifications and
estimates (professional fees can be included) all in duplicate. Needless to say the documentation needs to be clear enough to show exactly
what you are proposing to do. And the council will check that the
cottage is actually yours. A grant will normally be paid when the work
is completed but a council may be willing to pay by instalments as
work proceeds. Either way, payment will only be made if work has
been carried out to the council's satisfaction. Don't forget your tradesmen will still need to be paid by you on time—you may have to ask the
bank to act as a buffer.

Other conditions? Well, an owner-occupier must certify broadly
that he intends that the cottage will be his only or main residence and
will be occupied exclusively by himself and members of his
household; grants are not available for cottages used as second homes
or for holiday letting. (I hope you don't think I just mix with villains but
it has been known for lies to be told—a teenage child has been known

to make an application before now, as the 'owner' of what was in fact a second home. I am not condoning such activities, just pointing them out in the relentless search for truth.)

You may qualify for a grant if, as a landlord, you are renovating a cottage to let on a residential basis but that poses all sorts of other problems which are dealt with later in the book.

I've always been in too much of a hurry to apply for grants (and too scared of having to meet onerous conditions) but it is worth investigating further before you start work. By the way, a council may want to see quotes for the work before making a grant; however, they are not likely to insist that you actually use a builder who gives you a quote nor that you have to accept the lowest estimate. Indeed you may be able to have the work estimated by someone then have the job done as you wish, eg by day work. The authority will only allow what is reasonable anyway.

Incidentally, if you have the joy of owning a Listed Building, you may be able to get additional grants. Note 'may': you are not automatically entitled to anything. Forgive me if I clamber on a hobby horse for a moment, but if you hit what you feel is an unreasonable impasse over grants then don't hesitate to kick up a fuss by writing (or threatening to write) to MPs, ministers etc. A friend got trapped in Catch 22—he couldn't get a mortgage for a cottage until he could prove he had grant aid towards the repairs; he couldn't get a grant until he could prove he had a mortgage. The solution? A series of letters to local authorities and an MP. If you come across a problem like this, even threaten the ultimate sanction in our crazy world of writing to The Media. But do be sure the impasse is unreasonable otherwise you will be dismissed as a crank.

Insurance

Having bought your cottage and, hopefully, obtained a grant towards the cost of renovation, do cover yourself by taking out a proper insurance. You *must* be protected, in fact people lending you money will insist that you are and may stipulate that 'their interest' in the place is recorded on the policy. Make sure that your insurance cover keeps pace with inflation. Insure for the 'full rebuilding cost' remembering that this keeps rocketing and that, for instance, special windows and doors for old cottages will be costly. Insurance comes at the end of the cottage-buying saga, when you may be drained emotionally and financially. As a result you may tend to under-insure, on the theory that 'it will never happen to me'. Every day it happens to someone. And don't forget the contents of the cottage when insuring. You should have a 'new for old' policy otherwise you won't get your worn items replaced by brand new ones if you have a fire, flood or whatever. Shop around—insurers for houses may not be the best for contents. While you are renovating you may only be able to get fire insurance because obviously, if the cottage is wide open, people are unlikely to give you cover on the contents. If you are leaving a second home empty during the winter there may be other conditions. Some companies exclude damage by vandals while a place is unoccupied and you will almost certainly have to guarantee to drain water systems during the winter; not unreasonable to avoid burst pipes.

Fire precautions

I always think fire is more frightening than frost; it makes sense to take proper fire precautions with your cottage. And remember that you can do almost more damage with the wrong fire-fighting equipment than by leaving a place to burn while you call the fire brigade.

A long chapter, I fear, but money is important. Anyway there you are; a nervous wreck and nearly bankrupt *but* the cottage is yours at last. Take photographs of it to look back on later and as you plan your renovation remember what William Pitt said, speaking on the Excise Bill: 'The poorest man may in his cottage bid defiance to all the forces of the Crown. It may be frail—its roof may shake—the wind may blow through it—the storm may enter—the rain may enter—but the King of England cannot enter—all his force dares not cross the threshold of the ruined tenement!'

Mind you, they didn't have VAT men in those days.

6

Planning the Changes

In your first flush of enthusiasm once the cottage is yours, don't start tearing out windows or demolishing walls. Instead, sit and think because proper planning at this stage will save time, money and your marriage. If the cottage has been up for 100 years or so it will survive for another two or three weeks while you think about what you want to do. *Above all, don't rip out old features unthinkingly; we destroy our heritage too readily.* Go round your cottage with a notebook and list what needs attention. This is important because you will soon become used to things; if something jars when you first see it, say, a hideous modern sundial, then make a note because after a while you will become accustomed to its face. It helps if you can live in a place for a while before knocking it about as this may mellow your initial ideas. In one house, we rushed to replace leaded windows to let in more light, then a year later we enlarged several windows, so the first operation was a waste of money. Poor planning.

Advertising brochures, available by ticking pages at the back of DIY magazines or the glossy house monthlies, may be helpful, for instance kitchen and bathroom leaflets usually have planning suggestions in them. A building supplier's catalogue will guide you on material prices, while if yours is a very small cottage, study caravan magazines for ideas on squeezing quarts into pint pots. If there is a similar cottage to yours converted nearby, ask to view it to get further ideas.

If your renovation is to flow smoothly, you need to be organised, so have a home office or filing cabinet. Keep copies of any letters you send and file all documents you receive; obtain receipts wherever possible because they may affect what you can claim against tax later.

If you have time, try to trace the history of your cottage because it will add to your enjoyment of it. Local records offices may have old

Figure 13. *The cottage shown in* Figure 5, *part way through its renovation. If you have the choice of cottages in a terrace, pick an end one because you will be able to add windows to improve lighting and ventilation.*

pictures; ours dug out 50-year-old sales particulars of one cottage, which made fascinating reading.

Let me repeat: stop and think before you do any renovation. You may feel that having bought the place you can do what you like with it, including knocking the outside about, but think carefully before changing the appearance. Of course, some change may be essential; I am not suggesting you should revert to an open fire in the centre of the floor with a hole in the roof, nor should you have to trip out to an earth closet. But try to keep external changes in sympathy with the age of the cottage and its location. If your cottage is in a terrace you need to be particularly responsible because one oddball can ruin a whole row; a single pebble-dashed cottage in a row of Yorkstone ones can spoil an entire street. Try not to convert a cottage so that it looks self-consciously attractive and don't convert one out of its price class. If you are amid £40,000 cottages and spend so much on a conversion that yours ends up costing £70,000, you may have difficulty in recovering the full amount if you sell. Classic conversion faults include taking down chimneys (thus destroying the balance of a roof line); replacing old tiles with modern concrete ones; installing badly proportioned windows and rendering over attractive old brickwork. The possibilities are awful and endless.

Keep in mind the question of maintenance in your planning. Tile-hung cladding on an outside wall will be cheaper to keep fresh than wood facing; an inside wall left in natural brick can make an attractive feature and will be cheaper to maintain than an emulsioned or wallpapered wall. Beware of oddball features; out-of-character pargetting showing a flock of ducks in flight may not add to the charm or value of your cottage. If you need more space in your cottage, you may consider adding a ready-built extension. Most manufacturers of these will help with planning and finance but flat roofs for extensions rarely sit happily with cottages (they were probably unheard of when your place was built). If your cottage has a lot of higgledy piggledy roof lines, try to keep them if you can because they will be part of its charm.

Inside thoughts

Having given some thoughts to the outside appearance, move inside. Here you have more freedom to modify things, although try not to end up with the interior totally at variance in style with the outside. Get some squared paper, a ruler—preferably a plastic one which you can see through—pencils and a rubber. Make a rough plan of the cottage and don't show walls as just single lines—remember they are quite thick. Show which way doors open and mark which walls are load-bearing. (It could be worthwhile having a floor plan done pro-fessionally even if you intend to draw any other plans yourself.) Plans are usually drawn on a metric scale of 1:50 or 1:100. Metrication has struck in the building world harder than anywhere else; we really need an Imperial metre which is the same size as a yard.

Note which way rooms face. Those facing south should get more sun than the others although you may have little choice in how to utilise rooms in an established property. I think you need to take care when changing the normal use of rooms; it is possible to convert a bedroom into a lounge to make the most of a view, putting your bedrooms downstairs, but these arrangements can be off-putting. Surrounding noise could affect your planning—if you are opposite a pub (lucky devil) then you may decide to put children in back bedrooms. Don't feel locked into keeping the kitchen where it is, simply because drains are already there. New drains are relatively expensive but not so much that you need suffer the constant inconvenience of a kitchen or bathroom in the wrong place. Keep in mind that with a mechanical

Figure 14. (Left) *A typical old cottage layout with a third bedroom leading directly off the second.*

Figure 15. (Right) *When we renovated the cottage shown left, the small bedroom was turned into a bathroom; the stairs were switched round; a window was put in the end wall and a new studding wall made bedroom No 2 self-contained. The position of the bedroom door on the new wall was critical to provide enough length of wall to put a single bed along it.*

vent you can have them inside the cottage without an external window.

One of the simplest ways of adding more space may be to convert an attic or you may be able to slot a gallery into the end of a lofty room as a second storey. If there is enough space in the loft then an attic conversion may be cheaper than adding an extension and will not use up any outdoor space; in addition, you don't need planning permission unless you are adding a roof extension or a dormer window. Key ques-

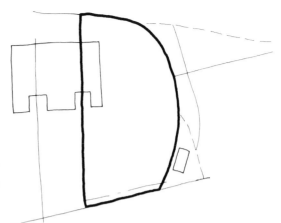

Figure 16. *A block plan like this shows the position of a property on its site. You will also need a location plan showing where the site is in relation to the sur- rounding area.*

tions when planning a loft conversion are: will there be enough head- room and will the existing joists be strong enough? *Don't* auto- matically rush to one of the heavily advertised national loft conversion specialists—once the plan is sorted out the work itself is not difficult and will be within the reach of local builders or even the DIY man. I tackled a loft conversion once with tongued and grooved panelling and coped reasonably well; in fact friends commented that the diagonal panelling had rather a unique character.

If yours is only a small cottage, decide if you really need a formal dining room. Perhaps a gateleg table in the living room would make more use of the available space? Open plan arrangements do not always look right in old cottages, nevertheless consider merging two room functions into one by knocking down a wall, say, to make a large kitchen/diner, if the only alternative is two very tiny boxes. Place the dining area near to the kitchen if you can to avoid too much to-ing and fro-ing with dishes.

Spend some time at your cottage with a chair or old beer crate, a notebook and floor plan; sit in each room in turn and consider what you want to do with it. Establish where furniture will go. Think which way doors are going to open. Decide where you are going to keep pets. Is there adequate storage space and will part of it be tall enough for brooms and ironing boards? Will it be possible to pull beds out to make them easily?

Avoid too many different floor levels because they can be dangerous and also cause problems for the disabled. If you have someone who is disabled in mind when planning, get hold of *Designing for the Disabled* by Elwyn Goldsmith, available from RIBA Publi- cations.

Figure 17 (Above). *A side elevation of a conversion we did. The position of the new window on the left was critical —for convenience it would have been better further to the left but it would then have jarred with the join of the sloping roof above it.*

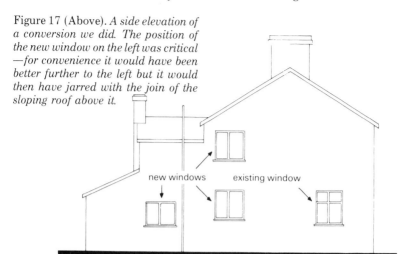

new windows   existing window

Figure 18 (Below). *The original floor-plan of the cottage shown in Figure 24. There was no bathroom and no room for one upstairs.*

Figure 19 (Right). *The old kitchen proved large enough to take a bath-room (and airing cupboard) while a new kitchen/diner was added to the rear. A front door was replaced in the lounge and an arch to the adjacent cottage was bricked up (both following a stab at renovation by a former owner).*

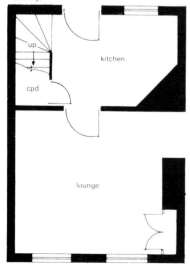

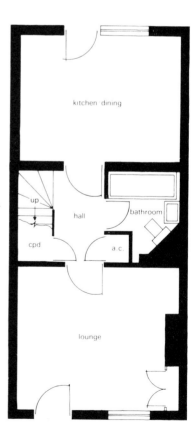

Getting advice

During the vital 'thinking' stage, don't be too proud to listen to other people's ideas—I've been fed solutions to tricky problems by plasterers and bricklayers working on adjacent properties who had renovated similar cottages to ours.

Of course, you may decide to take professional advice at an early stage by using an architect. Fees will depend on what you are having done and whether you want the architect simply to get the plans passed or to supervise the job through to completion. The best way to find an architect is via personal recommendation by a friend or, perhaps, a builder. Some readers may question why I put the builder before the architect and will argue that the latter should recommend the former. All I can say is that I've always started by finding a local builder first and I've never had problems. The defence rests. Instead of an architect, you may consider using a local draughtsman or 'build-

Figure 20. *Storage is essential in a cottage for ironing boards, vacuum cleaners etc, so don't be too keen to remove hall cupboards to install open plan stairs. The wall here is ready to be replastered following the insertion of a damp-proof course, while the door is away being stripped; note the damage on the side panel where a turn catch has worn it away over the years.*

ing consultant', ie someone who is unqualified. I have worked with four architects and five unqualified people (using the former for the more elaborate jobs) and have had reasonable service from all of them. In one instance a draughtsman thought of something an architect had missed, simply because he was interested in the area and knew about similar properties. Ask an architect or consultant to show you plans of other work he had done—this will give you an indication of whether or not your thoughts will be in harmony. Whichever category of adviser you use, go through the cottage with him room by room and discuss what modifications you have in mind. If your own ideas get a frigid response from an architect, remind him that he belongs to the profession responsible for the present London skyline and for high-rise flats. One can only agree with a Secretary of State for the Environment who commented that our generation does not deserve to be remembered for the quality of the architecture it will leave behind.

Beware of any consultant with grandiose plans who is trying to create a monument to himself (at your expense). You know more about your family and its lifestyle than any architect or consultant, so take advice (after all you are paying for it), but don't be brow-beaten into something you don't want. The more thorough the debate over the modifications, the better the result is likely to be.

At last you know exactly what you want to do to your cottage so it's time to start, isn't it? Well, er . . . I'm afraid not. You aren't finished with paperwork yet because you will have to get your ideas cleared by the local authority. Onward, ever onward.

7

Getting the Plans Passed

Unless the renovation of your cottage involves little more than a new coat of paint, you may need planning permission and/or approval under the Building Regulations; it is important to understand the difference between the two. Planning permission is concerned with the effects on other people of what you are planning to do. The various controls exist to regulate the development and use of land in the public interest; if they seem nit-picking at times, think how browned off you would be if a gravy factory was allowed to be built next door to your cottage.

Building Regulations are more concerned with ensuring that your cottage is safe against collapse, damp, rot and so on; that people living in it have proper toilet facilities, enough light and a safe staircase. Considerable emphasis is placed on fire control and means of escape in case of fire. All common sense; all controlled by the Building Regulations. Most building work (apart from normal running repairs) will require approval under the Building Regulations, irrespective of whether planning permission is needed. If you have any doubts, consult your local authority. Planning permission does not give you Building Regulations approval nor does Building Regulations approval give you planning permission! Therefore, in cases to which both controls apply you need both planning permission *and* Building Regulations approval.

Not surprisingly there may be confusion at times. You may get someone in a planning department telling you to use a certain style of window so that it remains in sympathy with the district, whereas someone in the building section will tell you to have windows of a different size to comply with statutory regulations! It's a full life. Because the regulations are so involved, you should get a copy of the DOE booklet *Planning Permission—A Guide for Householders* (available from your local council). Most architects and builders (and Building

Inspectors if they are honest enough to admit it) use unofficial guides to the regulations but, if the work you are planning is so complicated that you hit major problems, you should take professional advice.

Under the Town and Country Planning Regulations, various fees are payable for applications for planning permission or approval under the Building Regulations. As building costs rise so, automatically, will the fees but after all, why should the general ratepayer subsidise those of us who want to build or renovate? Your council will be only too eager to give you their detailed scale of charges.

You will not need planning permission to extend your cottage *provided* you can satisfy the following conditions:

1. The work must not increase the volume of the original place by more than whichever is the greater of:
   (a) 70 cubic metres which is approximately 2,472 cubic feet (50 cubic metres in conservation areas) or
   (b) 15 per cent of the volume of the original house up to a maximum of 115 cubic metres.
   For many old cottages instead of 'original' a more accurate description may be 'as the dwelling existed at (date)', with the date inserted after checking with the local authority.
2. The height of the subsequent building must not exceed the height of the highest part of the roof of the original house.
3. No part of the extension projects beyond the forwardmost part of any wall of the original house to face a highway.
4. The development must not be contrary to the condition of an existing planning permission.
5. The extension must not be for occupation as a separate and independent dwelling (so you can't let it as a self-contained unit).
6. The development must not obstruct the view of people using a highway used by traffic in such a way as to make it dangerous.

Complicated? Not if you take each clause slowly. And if you think the rules are restrictive, take heart from the fact that you can usually add good-sized rear kitchen or bathroom extensions to a typical cottage.

Tighter regulations apply in National Parks, Areas of Outstanding Natural Beauty and Conservation Areas so, for instance, it would be forbidden to paint just one of a row of natural stone cottages. Quite right too.

If the work doesn't fall under the conditions listed above then you need planning permission. From my experience you will find a local authority helpful over planning if you approach them in the right way so although you may not have tackled your own legal conveyancing, you may well consider applying for your own planning permission. After all, if you foul up your conveyancing you may end up in front of a judge, if you make mistakes on planning applications the authority can only throw them back.

You need to get a form from the council's planning department and at the same time ask if they have an explanatory leaflet to help you fill in your application (most of them have). You can prepare the necessary plans yourself (they don't have to be done professionally, the ones needed are listed on the form) but they must be sufficiently accurate and clear for the site to be properly identified and for the authorities to understand just what you are up to. An application 'must' be accompanied by four copies of an extract from a current OS Sheet scale 1:2,500 or 1:1,250 on durable paper showing the site boundaries edged in red together with adjoining buildings or parcels of land and any adjoining land owned to be edged in blue'.

It may be helpful to call at the planning office to discuss your proposals before you complete an application, although views expressed by officers will be given without prejudice to any decision which may be finally made by the council.

By the way, you don't have to be the owner of the land to which the planning permission relates, although you must inform the owner of what you are doing. This would apply if you bought the cottage 'subject to planning permission for such-and-such'. It helps if you know when planning committees meet so that you get your application in on time. Be pleasant to the various officials you encounter—they are only doing their jobs and you will get better service if you treat them as human beings. But don't carry kindness to the point that you get browbeaten or are given the runaround; if this happens, kick up a fuss.

If you are thinking of doing part of the renovation now, then further work later, it will be sensible to put all the plans in at once to save the time and cost of a further application; remember that there is a time limit on planning permission so if you dither for years before starting, you may have to re-apply.

If you have not received a decision within eight weeks of submitting documents for planning permission you should call the planning department. If they are having problems, either with workload or peculiarities affecting your application, they may ask you to agree to an extension of time. Allow this if you can, although you can in theory appeal to the Secretary of State on the basis that the authority has in effect refused your application.

I know all this sounds complicated and you may think it is an interference in civil liberties, but don't winge and whine. The Lord Mayor of London was controlling the construction of privies way back in the twelfth century and anyone who has travelled in a country with few planning restrictions will be more than sympathetic towards the laws of Britain. If you are tempted to bypass the system remember that you can be forced to demolish a place if you go too far without permission. Yes, a cottage can be compulsorily demolished. It couldn't happen? It has happened recently to two very expensive conversions within 20 miles of where I write.

Listed Buildings

There will be further restrictions placed on what you can do if your cottage is a Listed Building. The Secretary of State for the Environment and the Secretary of State for Wales are required to compile lists of buildings of special architectural or historic interest—hence the name. Any building built before 1700 which survives in anything like its original condition is listed. Most buildings between 1700 and 1840 are listed by selection; between 1840 and 1914 only buildings with definite quality and character are listed. Finally, between 1914 and 1939, selected buildings of high quality are listed. Grade I buildings are of exceptional interest (only about 2 per cent of listed buildings are in this grade) while Grade II are buildings of special interest and warrant every effort to preserve them.

The fact that a building is listed as of special interest does not mean that it must be preserved intact under any circumstances, but it *does* mean that it must not be demolished unless the case for it has been fully examined, while any alterations must preserve the character of the building as far as possible (which can be costly). If you own a Listed Building you must obtain Listed Building Consent from the local planning authority before demolishing it or altering it in any way. The procedure is similar to that for obtaining planning permission and details can be obtained from the planning department of any county or district council. It is an offence to demolish or alter a Listed Building without consent; the penalty can be a fine of unlimited amount or up to 12 months' imprisonment or both. I reckon offenders should be deported. If your application for Listed Building Consent is turned down, or granted subject to what you consider onerous conditions, you have a right of appeal to the Secretary of State.

Incidentally, if you fail to take reasonable steps to keep a Listed Building in good condition, the local authority is entitled to buy it compulsorily or, if it is unoccupied, to repair it and recover the costs from you. If you deliberately neglect the building in order to redevelop the site—it has been known—the local authority may not only acquire the building but may do so at the price which *excludes* the value of the site for redevelopment.

Anyway, whether the building is listed or not, if you have submitted your plans properly and exercised due patience, you may eventually receive a formal 'notice' full of legal jargon about this Act and that Act—ignore the jargon because what matters is that the plans are passed.

Appealing

Sadly, planning applications don't always succeed. We have a small building, which was once a guardroom, standing on the site of an old house in a third of an acre which would make an ideal small cottage. After our first, fairly simple, planning application was refused, we submitted a dressed up version with more elaborate drawings and stated that it would be used as accommodation for an elderly relative, my mother-in-law in fact (upon such sacrifices . . . the gods themselves

Figure 21. *An old guardroom, ideal for conversion to a small dwelling but, unfortunately, forbidden by the planners.*

throw incense). It didn't work. We were told that not only does the site
'lie within a Conservation Zone of regional significance because of the
variety of its flora and fauna', the planning authority also felt that:

> The proposal, if permitted would result in the consolidation of the
> existing sporadic development remote from any village centre and
> would be injurious to the appearance and character of this rural
> locality.
>
> The local planning authority do not consider that the proposed dwell-
> ings is/are at the present time, essential for the needs of agriculture or
> that the personal needs of the applicant outweighs the planning objec-
> tions to the proposal, as set out above.

We took advice from Queen's Counsel and were advised not to bother
appealing. (There's a free coconut for any reader who has any bright
ideas about how we can gain planning permission.)

Anyway, if you need to appeal, get a copy of the DOE booklet *Planning Appeals—A Guide to Procedure* from your council. You have to
appeal within six months but, before you rush off, talk to the local
planning authority because it may be possible to come to some com-
promise by altering your proposal slightly. Incidentally, over the past
few years about a quarter of appeals have been successful.

Remember that even if you get planning permission you still have to
consider the Building Regulations. If you are going to get embroiled in
these yourself, rather than through an architect or building consultant, then buy a copy of the Regulations from HMSO and grind
through them as well as the accompanying explanatory manual; there
are also 11 'Approved Documents' which cross-refer to the various
Regulations and suggest methods you could use to comply with them.
However—and I'm sorry to be the one to keep bringing you bad
news—you can't just browse through the Regulations, do the renovation and then move in. It is a little more formal than that because
you must have the work inspected either by the local authority's
inspectors or, in theory anyway, by a private approved inspector;
either way you will have to pay (of course). I say 'in theory' because
there don't seem to be too many private people operating as approved
inspectors at the moment, possibly because of problems in getting
insurance cover.

You can either submit full plans *or* a Building Notice with simply a
site plan and just enough detail for the authority to see what you are
planning to do—and perhaps more important, what you are *not* planning to do, such as build over an existing sewer. The Building Notice
method involves less work but more risk because if what you do is

later found to be wrong you will probably have to put it right; obviously this is less likely to occur if detailed plans have been approved before you start. There have been cases where people have got in a muddle and had to stop work under the Building Notice system so I'd be inclined to submit full plans. But it's up to you—I can only hold your tiny hand so far.

Caution: if you need planning permission as well as approval under the Building Regulations, don't steam on once you feel you are through the latter—you still need the all-important planning permission and this may take time to come through.

When you eventually start work you—or more likely your builder—will have to advise the inspector when certain stages of the work (drains, damp-proof course etc) are ready to be checked, then leave the work open for inspection for 24 hours after notification; it is an offence to cover any stage of the work before this period expires. The building inspector has the right to come on site at any other time he wishes to see that the work complies with the regulations. If you come up against difficult working conditions which might justify special inspection procedures, then contact the planning office who should be able to help (if approached properly). Sounds complicated but it isn't really and builders take it all in their stride.

Do remember that a building inspector checks that the work complies with the regulations, he does *not* act as a quality controller so don't expect him to perform in this role if you do the renovation yourself; provided the foundations and damp-proof course are done properly, he will not be unduly bothered if the corners of an extension are not at 90 degrees!

Let us assume that you have full approval to convert your ramshackle cottage into a palace. It is now time to move away from paperwork and on to more practical things.

8

Doing the Work

Thinking of doing the renovation yourself? Well, if so, don't be seduced by the apparent ease of it all as portrayed in glamorous ads in house magazines with attractive couples effortlessly painting Sistine ceilings in their cosy little semis. Such ads make DIY seem like a modern fertility rite. It isn't like that in real life, not in our house anyway. DIY needs marital understanding; working on a cold cottage in the middle of winter is one of the least effective aphrodisiacs I know.

Above all, accept that if you do the renovation yourself you will have to *work*. When your friends go off to the pub or to play golf you will have to steel yourself to go painting. Just console yourself with the thought that you will get the same exercise, but with perhaps more long-term profit. Ease the strain a little by deliberately planning the odd weekend off as a complete break, otherwise you will get sick of the sight of the cottage and lose enthusiasm. If you do have a weekend off, don't go to an old National Trust ruin or Stonehenge (it will all be too much like your cottage); instead, go to the old Covent Garden to see how a well planned renovation can really work.

Clearly, there is no magic about many of the jobs involved in renovating a cottage; ultimately, of course, the entire nation will be addicted to DIY simply because of the insidious effects of children's television teaching our offspring how to build mansion houses out of used matchsticks. If you feel you have the energy, enthusiasm and organisational ability (and can keep your priorities right) then don't be scared of having a go yourself. Provided the work is not too complicated, DIY can be therapeutic; knocking hell out of a wall is very satisfying if you have had a rough week at work, while the joy of finding that you can actually do simple plumbing will make you feel ready to attempt brain surgery. With the variety of DIY tools and materials available, no one should be afraid of tackling such things as fitted wardrobes, cupboards, shelving, painting and so on. And consider loft insulation; all you need is a pair of gloves, a mask, time and patience—so why pay someone else to do it?

But, and it is a big 'but', don't underestimate the skills involved nor the time it will take if you do-it-yourself; a number of seemingly small jobs can add up to several days of work. Home wasn't built in a day.

If you decide to go ahead and do the renovation yourself, then you need not go short of advice. If a friend has done any DIY, he or she will be happy to tell you all about it—at length. DIYers are actually more boring than those who have given up smoking or started a diet; which is why people may edge away if they see remains of emulsion paint under your fingernails. More helpfully, there are 550 organisations in the construction industry which will provide information to a greater or lesser extent. Some of these trade associations seem to have short lives before being merged with other associations; others are clearly fronts for vested interests. Nevertheless, from my experience in writing to them, most are efficient in turning round their mail (more so than many other industries) and the quality of their literature is high. Incidentally, government departments were quicker to reply than private ones. Let us bush the good wine.

One organisation you'll hear about is the Agrement Board which is sponsored by the DOE and has representatives from the British Standard Institute, the Building Research Establishment and so on. The Board tests products in the building world and issues 'Agrement Certificates' giving an independent opinion on performance. The Board also produces publications on such things as cavity wall insulation, chimneys, damp-proof courses, roof materials etc.

If you have a cherished building and run into a complicated problem, which your builder or friends are unable to solve, keep in mind that the Building Research Establishment has an advisory service on building matters where they may have special knowledge (a fee is charged unless the information is very readily available). Further help may come from the national register of craftsmen (and women) compiled jointly by the Crafts Council and county planning departments—it lists people with the right knowledge and skills to work on old buildings.

If you are being really scientific in your planning, you can contact the Meteorological Office for averages of temperature and bright sunshine statistics in your area so that you can plan which time of the year to do the renovation (or just ring my publisher to see if my corns are bothering me).

Although there is all this weight of professional advice around, the enthusiasm and initiative still has to be sparked by you. If possible, browse round a building centre for ideas and read *Handiman Which* which should be available at your local library; it tends to overdo things, telling you more about fungi removers than you really need to know, but if you concentrate on the conclusions they may steer you clear of poor products. A worthwhile investment will be one comprehensive book on building processes and techniques. I've found the *Reader's Digest DIY Manual* useful; it's an elaborate publication, covering everything from knocking in nails to treating your damaged thumb when you've hit it with a hammer.

Mind, having read all the relevant literature, *don't get over-confident*; have the sense to use professionals where necessary or where your own lack of knowledge would mean the job would take too long or worse, be dangerous. So think long and hard before doing your own electrics.

What you tackle yourself will depend on your own skills but digging trenches is obviously not skilled work (just backbreaking). Painting is easy, while plumbing seems easy but one fiddling little junction or bend can take forever. Bricklaying is perhaps the most forgiving job—if you cut a pipe, wire or piece of wood too short then you have wasted it, whereas if brickwork doesn't quite line up then you can dab on a bit more mortar. Care though: brickwork is highly visible and if you do it badly it will haunt you forever. Good carpenters tend to be in short supply by the way, so consider a night school course in carpentry if you are planning to tackle a cottage in a year or two.

You may decide to do the work by 'direct labour', ie hiring individual trades and skills as you need them. This could be cheaper than giving the whole job to a builder but you need to be reasonably near to the property, you need organisational skills and you must be prepared for a lot of frustration and phoning. You will have to co-ordinate the various trades too; in this book heating is covered after kitchens and bathrooms, whereas in real life they would be taken together with pipe runs, radiator positions and so on to be planned.

Subcontractors will be interested in getting the job done and getting paid and they may need spoon feeding; if you haven't supplied material or equipment that they would automatically get when working for a builder, then they may be up up and away with consequent delay. In addition, they will not have any real interest in the cottage itself and are unlikely therefore to come up with constructive suggestions (as I've found small builders ready to do). At least supervising the work yourself will teach you some of the building trade's jargon. I

Figure 22. *Don't become alarmed as the early stages of renovation get messy— order will prevail eventually. Note the scrap door used as a bridge for wheelbarrows.*

was alarmed to hear of 'fixes' and thought I was employing junkies—
I've since found out that the main addictions in the building trade are
Radio 1, crisps (the empty packets are left all over the place) and
strong shag. In fact, the first 'fix' is when the carcassing timber goes in
(floor and ceiling joists etc) and the second is when skirting boards,
door surrounds and so on are fitted by the carpenter.

What is the difference between a carpenter and a joiner? I wish
you'd never asked. I've found different meanings put on the words in
different parts of the country but, broadly speaking, the joiner is the
more skilled and could if necessary make a sash window, whereas the
carpenter would do the woodwork involved in the roof structure etc. A
joiner could do a carpenter's work but not necessarily vice versa. In a
small building firm you may find that one man does both jobs, plus the
general bricklaying and other jobs too. If you spot such a paragon get
hold of his address because he will be the man to approach for general
tidying up work later in the renovation.

You will also learn at first hand all about the black economy. I've
never resorted to it myself (it says here) but you may have to accept
that some people will only do work if they get part, or all, of their
money in cash. No use tut-tutting about it—it happens and only a
change in the income tax laws will stop it.

If you have people working for you on your cottage, consider public
liability insurance. If scaffolding is left about and somebody falls off it,
you may be held responsible.

Safety

Which reminds me, *DIY can be dangerous.* People fall off ladders,
have accidents with paint strippers and other chemicals (which should
all be kept out of reach of children); they cut themselves with saws,
while the dangers when doing electrical work are obvious. Consider
your own state of health too; children and indeed adults with
asthmatic tendencies can be affected by fumes from paints (so keep
rooms well ventilated and wear a simple mask); if you've led a seden-
tary life, lifting paving slabs or even holding a 5 litre tin of paint for
long will come as a shock to your system.

Always wear strong shoes to protect your feet against nails in old
timber or something falling on your toes. Use eye protection when you
are chipping at plaster or brick and if you are making a lot of dust, wear
a face mask.

Take particular care if you decide to demolish, say, an old outbuild-
ing yourself. Start at the top and work down; save what bricks and tiles

you can, and burn rotten wood as soon as possible.

You can buy belts and aprons with pockets to hold tools so that they are near at hand; I think it is unwisely tempting fate to carry chisels or screwdrivers pointed at the groin.

Buying materials

Doing the renovation yourself will force you into becoming your own purchase agent. Here the message is the same as for so many other aspects of buying and renovating: *plan*. Prepare detailed lists of the various things you will need, and don't skimp on quantities or you may run out of something part-way through the work. Using petrol to drive to pick up a few essential screws is not a cost-effective way of building. Next, scout for the best prices, coupled with reliable delivery. Catalogues from builders suppliers, mentioned earlier, will give you some idea of prices and you should write or phone local suppliers— get names and addresses from Yellow Pages. Builders merchants are professionals but not all of them are efficient and I've wasted many hours with them; it can be frustrating at busy times to queue for 20 minutes while someone buys 47p worth of assorted screws. Better to call at quiet periods or write to them. Ask for a discount because unless you ask, you won't get one. You may find that a local hardware store will give you just as good a discount as the bigger people if you tell them what you are doing and buy most of your material through them. Some manufacturers have a 'trade' range; go for them where the quantities you need justify it.

Order as far in advance as possible and have bulk deliveries if you have adequate storage. Try to obtain wood at least a month before you need it so that it can acclimatise. For instance, if you are panelling a room with tongued-and-grooved boarding, store the timber where it will be used to avoid shrinkage opening up the joints later.

Watch holiday periods when ordering things, otherwise you may have excessive delays and do look after materials because it is believed that, across the country, homes cost 10 per cent more than they really need to because of wastage, theft and damage to materials on site. Having left three cottages open for several weeks with a lot of movable material in them, without losing anything, I can only assume I've been lucky or there must be a lot of thieves about in other areas.

During the restoration you will need transport. Consider buying a van for the period of renovation then selling it afterwards, because this could prove cheaper than repeatedly hiring transport. Line the load-carrying area of a vehicle with hardboard or carpet because plaster and paint mark while nails scratch.

You may decide that to avoid a lot of travel, the best way to operate is to live on the site (you may have to, or rent somewhere, if it is your only home) either camping out in one or two rooms or, if you need something more substantial, in a caravan. You will normally be given planning permission for a mobile home for a specific length of time. It will be more pleasant if you can connect the van to water, electricity and possibly, drainage. If you need to buy a caravan, remember that a large one without a site may be worth very little; scour local papers as well as *Exchange & Mart*. If you buy a van, don't get side-tracked into renovating it (it's the cottage you are interested in, remember?). Just scrub it clean, accept it as it is and be prepared to scrap it when you move into the cottage. Incidentally, it may be wise to explain to your neighbours that the caravan is only temporary. When we lived in one we got very frigid looks until friends visited us in a (borrowed) Rolls-Royce which pulled us out of purdah.

Other points about doing the work yourself? Well, appreciate that it will be a dirty job—so wear old clothes. A large hat will save you a fortune in shampoo, and if you wear spectacles, use an old pair at the cottage because they will get scratched and covered in paint. I know they don't sit very well with the macho image of the building world, but plastic or rubber gloves will save your hands getting knocked about (if you're a plastic fetishist, of course, you will double your fun; I'm still hung up on liberty bodices).

Make a list of 'what needs doing next' at the end of each day while the horrors are still fresh in your mind. Maintain a single chart as a record, with the rooms listed down the side and the jobs to be done across the top, putting ticks as the work is done. Buy good quality tools; I broke three cheap stripping knives before buying a 'professional' one which, although it cost two and a half times the price of the others, lasted for years. Be strong willed in DIY shops, they can be as seductive for grown men as sweet shops for kids. Consider hiring major equipment—ladders, concrete mixers and so on. Finally, beg or buy a milk or beer crate—ideal to stand on when painting.

Builders

Perhaps I've painted such a dark picture of DIY that you have decided to employ a builder to renovate your cottage. Well, Dr Johnson said 'to build is to be robbed', but this suggests he was either a bloody fool or badly advised.

WORK LIST	KITCH.	DINING	LIVING	B1	B2	BATH.
SCRAPE WHITEWASH OFF CEILING	/	17	13	1	5	/
" " " WALLS	/	18	14	2	6	/
TOUCH UP PLASTER - CEILING	/	19	15	3	7	/
" " " - WALLS	/	20	16	4	8	/
EMULSION CEILING - 1st COAT	25	23	21	9	11	27
" WALLS - " "	26	24	22	10	12	28

Figure 23. To help your planning (and sanity) make a chart listing every job then tick each stage as it is completed. This example has had the jobs put in order of priority as shown by the small numbers; note for instance that plaster in B1 is given time to dry while B2 is done; such detail on the chart is not essential but it does force you to think through your renovation.

In my experience there are more good builders about than bad. I have worked with eight different builders in seven areas of the country with hardly anything in writing and not a major problem. There are cowboys around, certainly, but if you fall for a quote which is half of everyone else's, or employ someone of no fixed address, then you deserve all you get. Caveat emptor as they say in Barnsley.

Builders regularly top the bankruptcy table but consider for a moment; anyone, be he a bricklayer or plumber can start up in business and call himself a 'builder' but without any business skills he is as likely to go bankrupt as anyone else. More likely in fact. The established builders' bankruptcy record is no worse than for any other trade.

If you have commissioned an architect then he will find and negotiate with a builder for you, otherwise the best method of finding a good builder is by word-of-mouth. Ask around among friends and perhaps in local pubs near to your cottage.

To catch some of the flavour of the relationship between a builder and a client, try to get hold of The Honeywood File and The Honeywood Settlement, two books written long, long ago which make hilarious reading yet contain much common sense which still applies today.

Don't ask impossible things of a builder; a local jobbing man won't be the best choice to repair a stately home. Do, however, utilise any particular skills his men have—one builder I use has a very talented bricklayer so I've had three brick fireplaces built by him. As with architects, you will get the best work from a builder if you brief him properly and you *must* provide a clear and unambiguous list of the work you want done if he is to give you a sensible quotation.

If your renovation is an elaborate project, you may consider using a quantity surveyor for this process—a member of the Institute of Quantity Surveyors. He could prepare a Bill of Quantities from your drawings, ie a list of materials, labour and plant required to complete the job. This allows competitive and comparable tenders to be obtained, since every builder is basing his tender on identical information. If any alterations to the project become necessary later, a quantity surveyor could agree a fair price with the builder and would negotiate over stage payments. Surveyors have dropped mandatory scale fees so if you decide to use one, do get quotes.

Let me stress that I think you should only take this route if your cottage is a major project. With the average small cottage, if you have a reasonable amount of common sense (which you clearly have to be reading this book), then it is unnecessary to get involved with an elaborate chain of surveyors, architects and what have you. A good builder will probably be quite sufficient.

Obviously, building costs vary from place-to-place and from builder-to-builder so even if you have a particular rapport with one builder, it still makes sense to obtain two or three quotes. Large building firms may have several full-time estimators but smaller ones either do their own estimating or use outside estimating services; it costs a builder around one per cent of the total sum to obtain an estimate so don't ask builders to quote unless you are genuinely thinking of using them. Builders become weary of people asking for a quote just to show to a building society to get a mortgage, then doing the work themselves or with casual labour. Building societies are not interested in who actually does the work.

A specification for a builder to quote from, prepared by a professional, may run to several pages and be so detailed that there can be no ambiguity. If you draw up your own list it will probably be briefer but it should still make clear exactly what work you want the builder to do. Looking through one of my old lists, I notice the phrase 'make good around roof and paint'. That was altogether too vague and could have led to litigation but didn't, mainly because the builder had viewed the cottage before we bought it and knew exactly what we had in mind. Although my simple list was not really detailed enough, do consider that sending a formal Bill of Quantities to a builder will almost certainly result in your bill being higher. If the specification makes much play of 'use such-and-such a pipe; form four man-made bends with spacer clips at x centres', then your builder will price every item instead of, with a simpler spec, working out that installing a length of pipe will cost £x.

Incidentally, keep in mind the difference between an estimate and a quotation. With the latter, the price quoted will be the price you pay but if an estimate is, say, £1,000 and the work comes to £1,100, then you pay £1,100; in theory if it comes to £900 then you should only pay £900 but if you believe that then you should make sure your cottage has a wide enough chimney for Santa Claus to clamber down.

One other way of working out the cost of the work is to ask a builder to submit a list of what he will actually do against each item you have listed. To give you an idea of costs, get hold of one of the building books, such as *Laxton's Building Price Book* (published by Kelly's Directories); this spells out in minute detail just what various items and jobs cost—how much to fit door furniture and so on. Warning: don't let your family see it because they will want to be paid if they find out how much is quoted to emulsion a square metre of wall.

It is sometimes said that 'builders make their profit on the extras', in other words, they put in a low figure to get a job then bump up the

Figure 24. *An illustration of the awful effect of colour washing just one of a row of cottages, a process which also adds to maintenance costs. The cottage on the left is that shown in* Figure 18.

1. Remove wall and chimney between kitchen and coalhouse. Brick up coalhouse door.
2. Make good roof, including sloping roof
3. Make good woodwork around roof and paint
4. New guttering
5. New soakaway/s
6. Add new window in kitchen
7. New window in diner under stairs
8. New window upstairs to light landing
9. New floor in kitchen

			BROUGHT FORWARD	£	
2 No	Excavate for and construct Soakaways in positions as plan 1·50 m². deep!	@	48	£ 96	
10. M.	Excavate for and lay 100 mm drain pipe (seconds) on pea shingle	@	17·5d	175	
4. No	E.O for 100 mm bends	@	4	16	
2. No	Provide and bed in concrete R/W Shoes with vertical back inlet	@	30	60	
2 No	Make cement joint to 62 mm R/W pipe to shoes	@	1·20	2	40
				349	40

2. Provide and bed 4" dia. salt glazed
   trapped gullies with vertical back inlet
   and finished with 2" wide x 4" high
   concrete kerb.

3. Excavate for and build manhole 2'0" x 1'6"
   inside dimensions in 9" fletton brickwork
   in cement mortar render externally and
   fairfaced internally on a 6" thick concrete
   1:2:4 base and provide and bed 4" half-
   round salt glazed channels and channel bends.
   Bench up either side of channel in fine
   concrete.

Figure 25 (Above left). *If you know your builder well, a simple worklist like this (part of that for the cottage shown in* Figure 13*) may suffice.*
Figure 26 (Below left). *This is how item 5 looked when broken down by the builders' estimator.*
Figure 27 (Above) *A more detailed list for a builder.*

price of the inevitable extras. Some builders may operate in this way but it is too sweeping a generalisation to apply to all of them. If no agreement is made about extras, a builder is entitled to charge what the work is worth (what is known as a *quantum meruit*) but clearly there can be arguments here, so sort things out in advance. Don't tell a builder (or, worse, one of his men) to do such-and-such a job, however small. Ask instead how much it will cost *then* decide whether to go ahead. Unless you have a good relationship with your builder, confirm the work in writing. However carefully you plan, there will be extras and they can mount up however they are costed, so do allow plenty for contingencies. And allow for the dreaded VAT too.

Ask the builder to put in PC (prime cost) sums for certain things—bathroom suites, kitchen units and so on. More and more people are buying these from the bulk discount places; your builder won't mind although you must include 'installation' on his work list.

If a quote arrives from the builder covered in small print (possibly on the back), cross out and initial any clauses which you disagree with and point out to the builder what you have done, then negotiate if necessary. It may be difficult to get a 'fixed price quotation' from a builder if costs are inflating badly; if you insist on one, he will play safe and pitch it high. If you get quoted 'cost plus profit' for an item—for instance where a builder is unsure what he will find behind a wall removed and cannot give you a fixed price—then at least put a maximum figure on the work otherwise if you, say, renovate a magnificent ceiling on a 'cost plus profit' basis the job could bankrupt you. You need to trust a builder before turning him loose on the cost plus basis.

Establish what stage payments, if any, are required (they will depend on the time and the sums involved) and pay them on time, it makes for goodwill and will help your relationship if anything needs to be corrected later.

If your renovation proves more expensive than you had anticipated, try not to delete jobs which will cause a lot of disruption if done later. Think of the mess if, say, you remove stairs at a later stage having decorated the cottage, laid carpets, etc.

Time gentlemen, please

Allow plenty of time for the work; no matter what completion date the builder promises you, *it will be later.* Traditionally, builders take on too much work, knowing that some jobs may fall through or that they may be held up for supplies. Incidentally, if you fancy yourself with flow charts and do a critical path analysis of the renovation, do retain it in the privacy of your own home; don't let your builder see it—he will fall about laughing.

If nothing firm is said about time, then a job should be completed within a 'reasonable time' but obviously this will depend on the circumstances; bad weather could affect a job and you would then have great difficulty in suing a builder over a delay. A well judged and deliberate loss of temper at a critical stage may be the most effective approach if things are dragging on too long. Often the client putting the most pressure on a builder gets his job done first. Don't give the impression that you are too easy-going or you will be pushed to the back of the queue.

Spell out if you want things saved (such as old basins, firegrates and boiling coppers which make splendid plant holders), and if you have any interest in the history of your cottage, ask the builder to keep anything unusual uncovered—old letters or newspapers for instance. Establish the position over access for lorries and diggers so that you don't upset neighbours, and make sure topsoil is saved. Stipulate that the builder must cart away excavated material, for instance from the foundations, otherwise you may find yourself with a man-made mountain of soil.

Figure 28. *On this builder's invoice the original Prime Cost Sum allowed for electrical work was deleted and the actual cost (£230) included because more power points and so on were added as the work progressed. The PC sum for sanitary ware was subtracted because a suite was bought in a discount store (the builders' cost for installation was included in the main figure). Minor extras like those shown are almost inevitable in a renovation and a contingency must be built into your budget.*

GLEMSFORD 280446

F. G. HAMLIN
BUILDERS
LIMITED

ALTERATIONS & REPAIRS
DECORATING   MILL BARN, STANSTEAD, SUDBURY, SUFFOLK CO10 9AP
PLUMBING
HEATING

FARM BUILDINGS
CONCRETE FLOORS
& ROADWAYS
A SPECIALITY

29th July 1986

Sales Invoice No. TU/ 193 Re: Liston Lane

To all works as per our estimate...	£ 5703. 00
less: P.C Sum for Electrical works	270. 00
P.C Sum for Sanitary ware..	350. 00
plus Cost of Electrical works	330. 00
	£ 5413. 00
Extra: Boarding our bathroom wall	135. 00
Renewing living room window	142. 00
Adapting kitchen window	43. 00
New step to front door	36. 00
Repair front bedroom window	29. 00
New threshold to kitchen	30. 00
	£ 5828. 00
plus VAT @ 15%	874. 20
	£ 6702. 20

Directors F. G Hamlin J. A. Hamlin   Reg Office as above   Reg in England No 1055425   V A T Reg No 103 0124 53

The builder must have the latest copy of your plans, particularly if you modified them during the planning procedure; establish a place to leave notes for the builder and vice versa so that you communicate properly. Don't be fooled by all the initial activity as scaffolding shoots up and piles of sand appear; you will expect the work to be finished in a trice. Don't start arranging milk deliveries—the pace will slow after a while.

Don't sit on a builder's shoulders and don't give instructions to all and sundry when you visit the cottage. The key to success in working with a builder is goodwill on *both* sides, so don't bicker and nit-pick all the time. The builder is in charge of site supervision, not you, so deal with either him or his foreman. If you tell a labourer on site 'knock down that wall, Paddy', you may find that the upper floor comes down with it.

If you have a case of bad workmanship, first give the builder a chance to put it right, if necessary withholding a portion of the bill to cover the work. If it is a big firm, write to or telephone the managing director. If you are still not getting satisfaction you may find that the threat of a letter to a consumer programme or local MP will be effective. If all that fails, consult your solicitor. Keep in mind that an oral contract with a builder should be as binding as a written one although it will be a lot more difficult to prove. Don't despair, if you have selected your builder with care and briefed him properly, then there is nothing to stop the renovation flowing smoothly.

Now having completed a broad review of the buying and renovating process, let us consider various parts of a cottage in more detail.

9

Basic Structure – Outside

Attend to the exterior of your cottage before tackling the inside—
there is little point in decorating a room if rain cascades through the
ceiling. Before you start renovating the exterior, remember that the
original builder almost certainly used local materials because it was
costly and difficult to transport bricks and so on long distances with
primitive transport; you should try to use local materials too in order
to retain the character of the cottage. Do try to renovate your
cottage sympathetically.

The roof

When weatherproofing a cottage, start with the roof and work down; if
possible try to get the roof on (and glass in the windows) before the
winter. I get dizzy if I mount a high curb quickly, so I've always left roof
work and facia-board painting to builders; unless you have a good
head for heights I suggest you do the same. Some decorating firms
offer what they call a 'top hat service', ie decorating everything outside, above the ground floor.

If you take the DIY route, do keep reminding yourself that the roof
is the highest point of a building and therefore the most dangerous
because you have further to fall. Buy, borrow or hire a safe scaffolding
kit or substantial ladder—when working on a roof you need a ladder
with an attachment which hooks over the ridge. I prefer aluminium
ladders to wooden ones because they are lighter to haul about and
seem stronger.

The first task with the roof is to check that the timbers are sound;
replace any rotten or damaged sections. Treat the wood with preservative then felt, batten and re-tile. A rather brief instruction which
makes it all sound easy. Surprisingly, it is, *provided* you have a head
for heights and follow the instructions given by tile manufacturers or
included in DIY books.

Figure 29 (Above). *If you have a loose tile (as here) remove it, nail a strip of copper, lead or similar to the batten, replace the tile, then bend the protruding end of the strip up to hold the tile in place.*
Figure 30 (Right). *Not for the DIY enthusiast!*

If your roof needs less drastic treatment, do at least check that the tiles are firmly in place. Push any loose ones back, securing them either with a blob of special adhesive or, better, with a strip of lead or alloy (or anything which will not corrode). Don't push tiles back then nail through them to the batten because water will follow the nail through the tile and down into your cottage. If tiles are missing, take another one off to use as a sample and search for matching ones; you may find some lying around behind old barns and farm buildings, otherwise head for one of the demolition specialists. If your cottage has roof shingles then a coat of creosote will help preserve them.

Thatch's life

Of course, the dream cottage has a thatched roof. Three hundred years ago thatch was the most common roofing, being used in towns until it became too much of a fire hazard. It was inexpensive then, although it's not particularly so today. Thatched roofs have wide overhangs to keep rain off the walls, which can make rooms dark but people who live in thatched cottages find them cool in summer and warm in winter; in addition thatch helps to keep down noise.

If you are adding an extension and want it thatched to match an existing section, then the roof will need a minimum pitch of 50 degrees so that rain clears easily. Get the best craftsman for thatching you can find and don't be totally put off if the thatched roof on a cottage you are thinking of buying is scruffy—thatch can be patched and new pieces will soon weather to the same colour as the rest. But get a quote before you buy the cottage. Bear in mind that some authorities will not permit you to replace thatch with tiles.

Keep the roof clear of leaves after repairing the thatch because they encourage moisture to collect. Covering thatch with wire mesh will keep it in place and stop birds pinching it for nest building. There is a fireproofing liquid available which you should stipulate when the work is done, and it makes sense to have a generous sized hatch for easy access to the roof space should you have a fire.

Unless your wife is very good at macramé and has strong arms, I don't think a thatched roof is the place for DIY—a badly repaired

Figure 31 (Above). *The rear of the cottages shown in* Figure 24. *As originally found with derelict outbuildings.*

Figure 32 (Below). *Outbuildings demolished and foundations laid for a rear extension; temporary glazing in one bedroom.*

Figure 33 (Above). *New windows put in and simple kitchen/diner extension built half way up.*
Figure 34 (Below). *Nearly complete. Note the dips in the roof under the windows which were needed to give adequate headroom in the extension; they also relieved the rather 'heavy' effect of the extension.*

thatch has all the charm of a home haircut. Incidentally, if you have a thatched roof repaired or renewed, don't overdecorate it with fancy patterns; if you have pargeted walls as well, your cottage may look like a poodle ready for Crufts.

It is commonly thought that thatch is a lot more expensive to insure than a conventional roof; not necessarily so. A friend with a thatched cottage in Devon approached a London company and was quoted a very high figure for insurance. She contacted the same company's local branch in Devon and they roared with laughter and said, 'Londoners know nothing about thatch, we deal with it all the time.' They quoted a much lower figure. The moral is: shop around.

Because of the roof overhang, thatched cottages don't have guttering. If your place is unthatched, then while you are up in the air with your parachute, busy making the roof sound, stay up there and check the guttering. It is possible to repair cast iron guttering with mastic, but plastic guttering is relatively inexpensive and it may be a better investment to renew the whole system with this. If you used to enjoy playing with Meccano (you still do? I see) then you will find re-guttering within your reach but do follow manufacturer's instructions carefully. Mount plastic guttering firmly or it will creak, and don't forget to slope it so that water can run away. Avoid windy days when fitting guttering or a long length may act as a wind trap and send you hang-gliding before you are quite ready.

Incidentally, plastic guttering may not bridge long unsupported gaps. We had to retain a section of old metal guttering on one cottage to bridge across a window; we painted it silver to match the new plastic sections and it seems to be surviving. Downpipes should feed to soakaways rather than old tubs but although most people can use a spade I wouldn't try to dig the hole by hand, a mechanical digger will take minutes not hours; combine the job with others which may need the unit. You can throw old rubble into a soakaway hole but *not* soft garden rubbish as this will simply bed down and the soakaway won't function properly.

A final point on plastic guttering and piping—stick to the well-known makes because you may not be able to find an obscure brand if you need to modify the system after a year or two.

Chimneys

If you intend removing an old fireplace, and the chimney goes up through the cottage, it may involve too much costly structural work to take it down, so simply cap the top. It will be easier to remove a chim-

Figure 35 (Opposite) *and* Figure 36 (Below). *A soak-away and new guttering tidy up the rear of a cottage. Even if gardening enthusiasts retain tubs, they should still have drainage from them to soakaways. Some manufacturer should offer a two way valve so that water can be routed from a downpipe either to a tub or straight to the ground.*

Figure 37 (Above) *and*
Figure 38 (Below). *A dis-*
used chimney can either be
capped or taken down and
the wall bricked up—see
Figures 39 and 40.

Figure 39 (Right) *and* Figure 40 (Below). *The removal of the chimney reduces weight, improves water protection and removes any problem with old soot; however, it is more expensive and is easiest to do in soft jointed brick because the main cost is in cutting and bonding new brickwork into old.*

ney running up an outside wall although, again, it can simply be
capped. Instead of demolishing a chimney, you may be considering
adding one; if so, a prefabricated unit may be less than half the cost of
a conventional brick chimney, though much more difficult to harmonise with a cottage.

If you are retaining old chimneys then do have them swept. This is
essential if you are adding gas fires; you should also contact your local
gas authority for advice on things like chimney openings which can be
critical. Consider covering the tops of chimneys with wire mesh to
keep birds out. If your cottage has remained uninhabited for some
time, you may have a running battle with swallows and house martins
to establish your right of ownership. At least they won't take you
before a Rent Tribunal.

Walls

Now consider the walls of your cottage. If you need more bricks, say,
to block up a window or doorway, search for matching ones (back to
the demolition man) to maintain a uniform appearance (done properly,
the joins won't show after a few weeks' weathering). If you find spare
bricks lying around, they should clean up fairly easily because the old
mortar will probably be soft and will scrape off.

If you are worried about damp through an exposed wall, treat the
brickwork with a silicon waterproofing liquid which will act as a rain
barrier while still allowing the wall to 'breathe'.

You may have to render outside walls to get an even look if you have
blocked up several doorways etc but this will change the appearance
of your cottage and will involve more maintenance so avoid it if you
can. Rendering is not a cure for damp; in fact if water gets behind rendering the problem will get worse. If you have clay, cob or mud-and-
wattle walls it may be difficult to plaster them, inside or out, and you
will have to add a covering of expanded metal first. Don't render outside walls while there is frost about.

If the outside walls are already plastered, tap them to see if the plaster is properly keyed; if it isn't, there will be a hollow sound which you
will soon learn to recognise. If there are problems, strip off and renew
the plaster, otherwise it may fall away later (this applies inside the
cottage as well).

You may consider timber cladding a wall, but only do this if it will be
in sympathy with the rest of the cottage and keep in mind maintenance; I know plenty of excellent timber preservatives and stains
are available but they still take time to apply.

Still thinking of the outside walls, *pointing* should be kept in good shape; if it looks grotty, dig it out to about 12 mm and replace it with new mortar which you can buy ready mixed (dearer than mixing your own but a lot more convenient). If you want to age new mortar or brickwork, brush it over with water in which you have had manure soaking; for the first week or two you'll learn who your real friends are.

Foundations

Moving to the bottom of the ladder, have a good look at the foundations. If there are trees nearby and cracks showing in paths around the cottage, then pull the trees out—bear in mind you may need local authority consent—and kill the roots. Keep any airbricks clear— remove any leaves or rubbish.

The problem with the foundations is more likely to be from damp than leaves or trees. If there is damp—it may be most noticeable inside the cottage—check that it is not simply a case of earth build-up around the cottage over the years, covering the damp-proof course. Sadly, this is unlikely to be the problem and you may have to take more drastic action. Damp causes mould growths on wallpaper, curtains and carpets; it corrodes metal; it damages plaster and mortar; it encourages fungus attack on timber. Not nice at all really and damp can make a place impossible to live in.

Figure 41. *Keep airbricks clear of debris around a cottage.*

Houses built before 1875 were not required by law to have damp-proof courses, although yours may have had one added later. There are several methods of installing a damp-proof course ('dpc'). A continuous slot can be cut through the wall with a power saw, then a metal or plastic dpc inserted. This really only works on walls up to 9 in thick; obviously the dpc must extend over the full thickness of the wall otherwise damp will simply rise through the mortar joints. Then the electro-osmosis method is popular because it is easy to install. A 9 mm wide copper strip is set into a mortar joint at normal dpc level and connected to a copper clad earth-rod driven 4–6 metres into the nearby soil. The only visible sign of the dpc will be a small bronze junction box on the wall face. This process works with any thickness and material of wall. Under a third method, chemical injection holes are drilled into walls then waterproofing chemicals are fed in and permeate the wall material. Again, the wall thickness and type present no problem. There is a fourth method by which porous clay siphon tubes are inserted into the walls. So there are plenty of cures to choose from for your damp.

We put up with three winters of bad damp in a Yorkshire cottage (getting complaints from holidaymakers in the process) before we took professional advice. One reason we had soldiered on for so long was that when we mentioned that we had damp, the locals said, 'Of course you have, this is Yorkshire'. I've always found the 'Andrews Heat for Hire' people pleasant to deal with and asked one of their experts to visit our cottage with the appropriate meters. I thought the damp was because the cottage was unoccupied for long periods and that hiring a dehumidifier would cure it. Sadly, it was not so, as the expert made clear in his report:

> Moisture content readings in the walls varied from 100 per cent at ½ in deep and 2 ft 0 in high in the corner of the front bedroom to 30 per cent in the living room towards the front door and 50 per cent towards the corner all in the external wall. Moisture contents of 80 per cent–94 per cent were recorded in the rear external walls.
>
> As the source of the problem would seem to be the lack of a damp-proof course, it would be of little use to reduce the relative humidity in the cottage by the introduction of a dehumidifier until the basic problem is corrected.

With the problem diagnosed, we ploughed through fairly technical literature from several firms offering damp-proof coursing, then met a local builder who told us that three people in the village had had dpcs put in by one particular company. We knocked on a couple of doors and found general satisfction so we contacted the same firm, which specialised in the chemical injection process. Along with its quote, the firm sent plenty of technical information, together with an Agrement Board Certificate on the proposed injection system. This said: 'It provides an effective means of preventing rising damp and the replastering system is effective in limiting damage to subsequent redecoration due to soluble salts retained in the walls.' The chemical dpc cured the damp but (an enormous but) this method does make a mess—plaster has to be hacked off a meter high up the inside walls, which means the skirting boards have to come off, then holes are drilled every 6 in or so, which means there is dust everywhere.

The moral of the story? If you need a dpc, add it early in the renovation process. We were so satisfied with the injection method that we used it later in other cottages but this time we had the sense to do the work at the start of the renovation.

Doors

Let us move on from damp to doors. If there are too many entrances in your cottage, consider blocking one off; this will not only reduce draughts but also increase the usable area in a room.

Figure 42. *With a chemical injection damp-proof course, holes are drilled at intervals along the wall. The skirting boards here were replaced and the plaster taken off up to 1 metre high then the wall was redone with a specially treated plaster.*

If you have to replace an external door, do bear in mind that a modern one may jar with an old cottage. However, avoid the opposite extreme—an over-dramatic 'oldie worldie door' with black plastic studding and hinges—because it will look absurd in a small place. One feels that a large hound should be slavering behind such doors; in fact it's usually a chihuahua guarding a painting of the inevitable oriental lady looking slightly sea-sick.

You can buy various glass fibre columns, door surrounds and so on which may work if you want to match something on an old property, but don't add them for the sake of it—they can look as daft as Georgian windows on a Victorian cottage. Remember too, that plastic house letters and numbers were not invented when your cottage was built so don't scatter them all over the place. When renovating, do try to keep things like this (and door knobs, letter boxes, etc) in sympathy with the age and character of the place.

Windows

Swinging from doors to windows, one of the most dramatic changes you can make to a cottage is to let in more light, so consider unblocking any windows which have been bricked up; such windows are usually in the right places and when unblocked will probably make a cottage look more balanced.

If you are adding a new window do try to match the existing ones, which may mean having it purpose-built. However, don't go to extremes. If yours is a very ordinary cottage then it may not be necessary to go to the expense of matching windows on, say, a side or rear wall, if a standard range is a reasonable blend. (Your planning officer may have a different view, of course). Aluminium windows? You wouldn't, would you?

Glaze windows as soon as possible to protect the interior. Glazing is easy but it's not a job I relish although actually accidents with glass are surprisingly few—there are four times more home accidents on staircases than with glass—nevertheless still take care, particularly if children are around. Bear in mind that a very modern patterned glass may look odd in an old cottage. If you are staining, rather than painting new windows then use a coloured putty.

You will let in more light if you remove leaded lights and you may consider deleting window bars at the same time but don't leave very big panes without any vertical support—you may hit little local difficulties, like the wall collapsing. And *don't* do such modifications if they would destroy the looks of a cottage. I must admit I have knocked

Figures 43 (Above) *and* 44 (Below). *Traditionalists may complain but the cheapest way to repair a damaged and draughty window like this may be to replace it with a single fixed pane, provided there is another opening window in the same room. This window looked out over rolling fields—another reason for improving visibility.*

out the rotten frame of a small paned window in one cottage, and put in a single, large sheet of glass. This has given us less draught, more light and a glorious view and, as it is tucked away at the back, the only purists who will see it will be trespassing.

Flat angle brackets may be screwed on to strengthen a weak window, while gaps around door and window frames (caused by age) should be caulked (ie, filled) with a mastic sealer; if you fill them with plaster or mortar, the joints will shrink and open up again.

Incidentally, if you decide on a loft conversion, don't let a dormer window get out of proportion and dominate your cottage; a dormer will be less obtrusive at the back than the front. As an alternative, consider a skylight, although this won't improve headroom.

All the external doors and windows may need painting but this is covered in a later chapter, so wipe your feet and let us move inside the cottage.

10

Basic Structure – Inside

If your cottage has very poky rooms then you may consider removing a downstairs wall to make two rooms into one, but do think this through before turning someone loose with a sledge hammer—an open plan may not suit an old place. The way the joists run will affect the cost of taking down a wall. If a wall runs the same way as the joists, then you have no problem because it will not be load-bearing. If the wall you want to remove is *across* the joists then you will have to put in a beam of some sort to support the flooring above—you will need to leave (or build) pillars at each side to support the beam. Instead of totally demolishing a wall, consider installing a pair of wide doors between two rooms instead; this will be cheaper and can give you occasional privacy if needed.

Upstairs, you will often find that one bedroom in a cottage can only be reached through another. If you have space, pinch enough from one room to make a passageway so that each room is self-contained. An additional door will be needed but the cost need not be too high because the wall can be a simple timber frame covered with plasterboard; such walls are lightweight and so impose little additional load on existing structures. Bear in mind that the original building work was done in imperial measurements—modern plasterboard will be in metric sizes if you are trying to match up a panel. If you add a studding wall, use insulation material inside as a sound deadener, particularly by bathrooms or children's bedrooms.

A timber clad wall of tongued and grooved boards should be within the DIY skills of most people; such a wall will be dearer than plaster plus paint or wallpaper, but will be virtually maintenance free. Nail the boards diagonally through the tongue so that when you tap the next board in place, the nails are hidden. Use a short length of spare board to tap with your hammer, or preferably mallet, when putting each board in place so that you don't damage the finished surface. Use

Figures 45, 46 *and* 47 (Opposite). *Old cottages often have a cupboard off one bedroom which juts out over stairs. Removing such a cupboard will improve headroom and allow access to an outside wall for a small window to be installed which makes the stairs lighter and hence safer (worth the loss of storage).*

thin nails and drill holes for them if the wood is particularly fragile to avoid splitting it.

If you consider using a decorative board to panel a wall, you really need to see a full-size panel to get some idea of the overall effect because a tiny sample may look fine in a shop but large sheets could be totally overpowering in your cottage. Remember where any battens are so that you can hang cabinets and things on to something secure later.

Natural brick walls can sit well inside a cottage—retain any yours already has or think about adding one if you have to brick up a section.

Warning: during this stage of the renovation, you may disturb the regular runs of mice and rats (particularly if you modify any outside walls). Our best score—ten mice caught in two days.

Patching up plaster on walls is an easy DIY task but the result of plastering is highly visible, so unless you are a confident and competent operator, get a professional to do large sections or new walls. If you have one new wall plastered in a room of three old walls, ask the plasterer to use a wooden float, rather than a stainless steel one, because he will then get a rougher final finish to match the original walls. It is possible to hide poor plaster behind a false wall. In one cottage we added a polythene sheet barrier, then fixed treated battens to the wall with new plasterboard to finish. This hid damp which had penetrated an old chimney. Do keep in mind that this treatment hides damage or damp—it does *not* cure it.

You may decide to remove old picture rails while you are attending to the walls although you may regret your act if the room is high and you destroy its balance; anyway if you do take down the rails, plaster over the area carefully otherwise hollows will show, particularly if you wallpaper. When taking down picture rails, (or *any* timber for that matter) do *beware* of nails which, as well as sticking through the wood, may also stick through your feet. Care and stout footwear are recommended.

Stairs

Apart from adding or subtracting walls, the most dramatic interior change you are likely to make will concern the stairs. Many of the traditional old cottages needing attention have narrow, twisty and dangerous stairs. If you remove a wall to open up the ground floor of a cottage then you may well install an open flight of stairs which will add lightness and brightness but may be noisy, while you will be unable to

Figures 48, 49 *and* 50. *The cottage shown in* Figure 13 *had stairs leading off a dining room which were steep and twisty. They were removed and a new flight of stairs was installed—see* Figures 51 *and* 52.

Figures 51 *and* 52 (This page). *Renewing the stairs gave more space in the room below as well as access to an outside wall for a window. The builder panelled the underside of the stairs instead of using plasterboard in order to match the stripped pine doors in the cottage.*

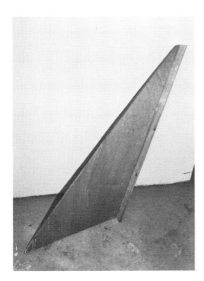

Figures 53, 54 and 55 (Below). *Instead of replacing poor stairs, consider rejuvenating them by nailing simple capping pieces over the old stairs. The parts of the old stairs which show here need staining or painting to complete the job.*

use the space below for storage (often at a premium in a small cottage). When planning the stairs, it will help if someone in your family is good at three-dimensional problems because working out how and where to get the right space may be quite a puzzle; in searching for a solution, try not to destroy the original character of a cottage's interior.

The Building Regulations covering stairs are not easy for the layman to follow. Very briefly, each 'going' (ie, the width of each tread less any overlap by the tread above) must be equal between consecutive floors. Each 'rise' shall be equal (if you think about the shock when you step on a stair that 'isn't there', you'll see the sense of this rule) and there must be a minimum of 2 metres headroom over a stairway. The key—and commendable—phrase in the 1985 Building Regulations is that 'stairways shall be such as to afford safe passage for the users'. However, the new Regulations are still settling down so if you are in any doubt about whether you can slot in new stairs, talk to a building consultant or architect—particularly if you are thinking of a spiral staircase. Don't despair if you haven't got quite enough headroom for new stairs because you may be able to pinch a bit from the room above; build the intrusion into some fitted furniture and it won't be noticed. By the way, a handrail is required for any flight of stairs more than a few steps high and one is required on *both* sides if the stair width exceeds 1 metre (this applies even if there is a wall on both sides).

If you have converted something like an old school or chapel and added a gallery, do make sure that there is a substantial rail along the edge of it for safety.

Ceilings

If the cottage has very low ceilings, then either bend your back (reminding yourself that the place has been like that for years) or dig the floor out to increase the room height; if this drops the floor below the ground level outside then you could get damp problems unless you remove the soil from around the cottage. If there are only three or four courses of brickwork below ground level you won't be able to dig down to increase ceiling height because the cottage may fall down (such cases occasionally make the national newspapers). It is possible to put new foundations under the walls *but* this will then make the structure less flexible and you would not be allowed to do this in, say, the middle of a terrace because one 'rigid' building would cause cracks. Lowering a floor is not a job to be undertaken lightly.

If conversely, the ceilings in your cottage are too high then consider a second ceiling lower down, which will make the place cheaper to heat although (as with removing picture rails) watch that you don't throw the proportions of the rooms awry. Strips of timber across a room with everything above them painted a dark colour will appear to lower the height. If you block off the top of a room completely, consider building in a hatch with a boarded area around it for storage.

Beams are traditionally associated with cottages and can look marvellous but they must look as if they 'belong'. Do have some respect for the original buiding when you convert—if there were no beams exposed, then don't expose any. Take your eyes away from the bottom of your glass and look around next time you are in one of the 'converted' pubs with fibreglass beams and you will realise the full horror of the genre. Very heavy beams may be overbearing; new, smooth-faced timber blackened to look like an old beam looks like new smooth-faced timber blackened to look like an old beam.

If a ceiling is in a very bad state of repair then ideally the old plaster should be stripped completely and new plasterboard lining fixed to the joists, but working 'upwards' on ceilings is not much fun so just patch the ceiling if possible, or get help.

If the results need camouflaging, you may be able to add coving which can be fixed with adhesive, provided the walls and ceilings are scratched to provide a key. But watch that coving does not throw the room out of proportion; it may look too ornate for a small cottage.

Fireplaces

Don't rush to block up fireplaces. With future fuel supplies perhaps uncertain, you may be glad of an open grate one day—the Clean Air Act would soon be repealed if energy got short. However, don't go to the other extreme and add a huge fireplace out of keeping with the rest of the cottage; a giant York stone one can overpower a small place.

Blocking up a chimney is relatively simple but do build in an air vent to ventilate the old flue and keep it dry and fresh. Consider building a cupboard into the grate space instead of bricking it up—probably cheaper.

Floors

Having sorted out the walls, stairs, ceilings and fireplaces, now continue downwards and check the flooring. First of all establish that you

have not bought an unexpected cellar (hopefully your vetting process will have revealed this). If you do have a cellar, clear it out and get it properly ventilated.

If the floorboards are in reasonable condition, sanding then sealing them with a polyurethane paint and using rugs may be cheaper than carpeting. Now is the time to do such sanding. Hire a machine and wear a mask; you may also need earplugs (as will your neighbours). If you have to take up floorboards—for instance for plumbing or wiring—mark them, otherwise you will have trouble juggling them back into place later. Where floorboards are excessively worn, shrunk or distorted, an existing floor can be overlayed with chipboard (use a 'flooring grade') which can also be used for a floor for an attic conversion by laying it on the original ceiling joists (after checking their load bearing capacity, of course). If your downstairs floor is wood and rotten, consider having a solid floor put in with a damp-proof course.

Having sorted out the walls and floors you can now finish trimming the house with skirting, although if possible delay this until the walls are painted. If you have had to remove all the old skirting downstairs while putting in a damp-proof course, it may not cost too much to renew it at this point. Plastic skirting is available which does not need painting but traditionalists will prefer good old fashioned wooden skirting. Carpenters seem to make skirting fit easily—I always end up

Figures 56, 57 (Opposite) *and* 58. *The simplest way to deal with an unused fireplace is to remove it (unbroken if possible so that you can sell it) then brick up the gap and plaster. Ideally this example should have had a rougher finish to match older plaster in the room. Note the gap left for an air vent.*

using Obo pins to get it to stay put, then I have to plaster fill where the corners don't meet properly. Nobody's perfect.

Doors

Think about the positioning of furniture before you decide where to put any new door openings. If you put a door in the middle of a new 3 metre long wall, you will not be able to put a bed against that wall; you will if the door is at one end. consider reversing the conventional opening of a door to make extra space in a room, but ensure that a corridor doesn't then become dangerous with doors opening into it. Avoid self-locking doors, ie where handles of opposite doors jam against each other. Folding or sliding doors may add space; glazed doors will add light but can look cold; louvred doors look smart but get very dusty and let noise and smells through. If you have to block up a door, consider putting a shelving recess in its place.

A sliding door may help if you are tight for space but otherwise use doors which are in keeping with the age and decor of the cottage. If you have old, painted doors, then consider having them stripped. Don't attempt to do this yourself with scrapers and paint removers, it will break your spirit. Instead, have them dipped in a caustic tank; if you

leave catches and hinges on, they too will come back paint-free. If you are going to change the position of door fittings remove them *before* having the doors stripped, otherwise they will keep the caustic fluid away from the timber and leave patches. If you take off door fittings, put them in labelled boxes or envelopes so that they go back on the right doors; renew the screws when replacing door furniture. When your cottage was built there were no such things as plastic handles, so don't use them. Use traditional door furniture and have it shot blasted if cleaning is necessary (rather than spending hours scraping) then paint it matt black.

I nearly forgot: it's worth checking around before having doors stripped because quotes vary wildly. If you take all the doors off to be stripped, leave them off until you have finished the decorating because it will be much easier to move about the cottage. There may be red patches on the doors after stripping where knots were treated, bleach will remove the marks.

When fitting a new door, nail a board about 1 cm deep on the floor across the opening as a threshold strip so that the door will clear carpets on either side. Renew other door bars if they have become worn over the years.

This chapter now takes a turn for the worse because it is time to consider damp, rot, woodworm and other intruders.

Figures 59 *and* 60 (Opposite). *A studding wall is fairly easy to construct. This one is being added to give privacy to the second bedroom shown in* Figures 14 *and* 15.

Figure 61 (Right). *New pieces can be spliced in to repair an old door as shown here by the hinge areas.*

Figure 62 (Below). *Old splash boards on external doors are likely to be rotten but are cheap and easy to replace, as here.*

Out, damp spot!

Don't panic over damp. The remedy may simply be good ventilation, particularly if the cottage has not been lived in for some time, but if damp persists then it must be cured (apart from anything else it brings on my gout). The main problem is that dry rot can develop wherever there is excessive dampness, so have a good prod around skirting and floors as well as in places like cupboards where fungi can spread without being noticed. Have a look around in the loft too.

There are two types of decay to be wary of, *wet* and *dry* rot. There is usually a surface growth with dry rot—white and like cotton wool when young, and grey strands when old (sometimes accompanied by reddish brown fruiting bodies). Timber appears dry and is often cracked both along and across the wood. Wet rot is more varied. Often there is no obvious fungal growth, although it may appear as black strands or white fluff. Wood usually looks black or dark brown and is soft and wet.

If you have the slightest suspicion that you have either sort of rot, get a survey by one of the many professional firms. Heave a sigh of relief if it proves to be wet rot, because once the rotten timber is ripped out *and the source of the damp cured*, you will be OK. If you have dry rot, you have more in store because if the fungus has spread through walls and behind plaster then the damaged timber will have to be replaced and the plaster will have to be hacked off over the infected area and for two to three feet beyond this—in all directions. Then the area will need treating with the proper chemical. All very unpleasant but if you don't make a thorough job of it, the rot may set in again.

We owe woodworm to the fertility of beetles which can lay up to 60 eggs at a time—this is all very commendable but unfortunatley they will persist in laying them in the cracks and crevices of timber. The grubs bore into the wood and eat merrily away. When the grubs turn into beetles they bite their way out of the wood, leaving their famous holes. They will return to lay more eggs. So when you see a hole and dust that's where a beetle has come *out*. Treatment? Well either get in experts or treat the cottage yourself with a proper fluid. Use a brush or spray, plus an injector (rather like the end of an oil can) to inject the killer into the timber via old fly holes, every few inches. Happily, excess fluid can be wiped off without causing damage to furniture or timber. When using chemicals for rot or woodworm do *read the instructions on the containers!* If you allow plenty of ventilation, wear protective clothing (particularly gloves) and take some fresh air at intervals, treating floorboards for woodworm is not too unpleasant. We found previous residents of one cottage had found an unusual way of dealing with woodworm in the upstairs floors—they had laid a second floor on top. We pulled this up before dowsing everywhere in killer fluid. We even feared we had woodworm in a door but our builder pointed out that what we thought were woodworm holes were in fact where a dartboard had hung.

When dealing with any of the rots or woodworm, burn waste timber as soon as possible.

During your renovation you may get problems with other intruders such as wasps, bees or ants; any garden centre will have chemicals available to kill these. I hate to use the word 'kill' but unless you are firm they may keep coming back.

On guard

One pest you are not allowed to kill–a burglar. I've usually had cottages in friendly villages where the custom is to leave doors open and I've never been burgled but you should consider making your cottage burglar-proof, particularly if you have any antiques. The first thing about security is to forget the idea that it can't happen to you; it is happening to somebody all the time. The local police will arrange for a free inspection to be made of your cottage and they will give advice on burglar-proofing. During the renovation you may consider installing a safe in a discreet place for your valuables, and when the property is yours and the builders have finished trooping in and out, change the front door lock. If you have been in the habit of leaving keys in a particular place for tradesmen, stop it. Old locks in a cottage are likely to be useless as security. Locks on outside doors should conform to British Standard BSS 3621/23 to be thief resistant. Ensure that doors are a close fit with surrounding frames (which will help to stop draughts too). A large barrel bolt may give you a false sense of security if it is held in place with tiny wood screws which would be easy to force. Similarly, if you mount a door chain, do so with strong screws and make sure the chain can't be snipped with a pair of nail scissors. If you have a glazed front door, put a letter collection basket in—it stops a telltale pile of letters on the floor indicating that you are out. Don't concentrate on doors then forget all about windows. Small key-operated window fittings can be an effective bar to burglars; double glazing makes their life more difficult, too.

As with burglaries, there is a temptation to think that *fires* won't happen to you, but as there are roughly 250 fires a day in Britain they must be happening to somebody. More than one fire in three occurs in the kitchen, although the majority of fires causing deaths start in a living room or bedroom—so give a little thought to your means of escape if you have a fire; very small barred windows in a tiny cottage can present a hazard. It makes sense to have a fire extinguisher in the cottage, installed in a convenient position. Keep it in good working order and *know how to use it* and in addition have a simple fire blanket available in the kitchen to smother cooking fires.

Finally, if you have a lot of timber in your cottage remember that although wood can't be made incombustible, its ignition can be delayed or even prevented if it's treated with appropriate fire retardant material. Keep in mind that many wood treatment fluids are highly inflammable, as are adhesives (such as for fixing floor tiles). Combustible vapours can hang around for several days so do take care with naked flames. We don't want to lose you.

11

Services

One of the earliest tasks when you start a renovation should be to connect the cottage to some or all of the mains services—water will be essential and you will soon need electricity connected, for instance most of the damp-proofing systems involve electric drills.

We can quickly deal with one service: gas. If there is no gas in the village then forget it. If the village has gas but your cottage is not connected to it, then you should go to your local gas board showroom and ask them to send someone to vet the place. They are obliged to quote for connection; there is no charge for their quote and there are no forms to fill in. If there is a local low pressure main within 25 yards they should be able to connect you; the gas people are not allowed to 'tap off' a medium or high pressure main.

Remember, by the way, that there are laws about gas safety. Natural gas is not poisonous so it has removed the main safety problem with the old type of gas. But you must still take care. In fact, so important is the safety aspect that British Gas can authorise officers to enter premises supplied with gas to inspect the installation and appliances, and they can cut you off if they think anything is unsafe. Want to stand on your dignity and prohibit their entry? They can get a warrant from a magistrate if they can prove it is necessary. So . . . only use competent people to install or service appliances; don't play about with them yourself. Gas is not an area for unskilled DIY enthusiasts; it is against the law to install or work on any part of the gas system unless you are competent. Use firms registered with the Confederation for Registration of Gas Installers (CORGI). If there is no gas in the area but you like it as a method of cooking and heating, then consider one of the bottled gas suppliers—with a tank installation outside you can have gas piped in for as many appliances as you want for heating and cooking.

Water, water anywhere?

With no gas, your dream cottage won't exactly crumble; you will be in much greater difficulty if no mains water is available. If your cottage has its own well then have the water analysed. If the report is gloomy (it will be) remember that previous occupants of your cottage probably lived to ripe old ages so swallow hard and carry on using the well unless the report is too alarming. If there is no well and your cottage is not connected to mains water, sending your wife to the village tap with a pitcher each day will delay your morning tea, so you really should get linked to the mains supply. Contact the local water authority, fill in a form and they will send an inspector to the site. The size of the quotation will obviously depend on how far your cottage is from the main. If the supply runs just in front of your gate you may get away with £100 or so. The cost will increase if the supply is on the other side of the road and the amount will then vary according to how wide the road is. The water authority connects to the boundary of the highway adjacent to your property, with a stop tap—or as most people call it, a stop cock. From there on, it is up to you.

If you are trying to run a water supply to a very isolated place, you will either need a licence from the highway authority to run a pipe along their road or an easement from the owner of land adjacent to the road to let you run a pipe in his ground (obviously cheaper than digging up a road to the nearest main. *But* . . . all this will not be cheap and you may get a weak water supply because of friction losses over a long distance, so check before you buy.

If your cottage is already connected to mains water, establish the run of the piping and in your renovation be careful not to interrupt your neighbour's supply—easy to do with old terraced cottages as one pipe often runs round the back supplying them all.

Flushed with pride

Moving on from water let us consider drainage.

Thomas Crapper, a Yorkshireman, really deserves a standing ovation because he was developing the modern WC system over 100 years ago. Nevertheless there are still plenty of places without modern facilities. If your cottage has the traditional 'privy' then you should read a little booklet called *The Specialist* which has all the folklore on the subject.

Portable chemical closets are, thanks to the caravan world, simple, efficient and quite acceptable but you will probably want to connect to the mains, if available. If the main drain is some distance away, talk to the local authority and sort out costs because connection could be expensive. If the area is not on mains drains, don't despair because a septic tank will be quite adequate provided you can get approval from the local authority (they will probably test water levels first). Tanks are available in concrete or glass-reinforced polyester and there are no moving parts to maintain—waste flows into the septic tank, then through a series of baffles where solids settle and can be taken away every so often by cleansing contractors under a local council service (for which you pay). The clarified water goes out through drains (typically in a herringbone pattern) which means tearing up a lot of garden. Septic tanks must not be within 15 metres of a habitable building—some local bylaws may stipulate greater distances or impose other restrictions (which may mean approaching adjacent landowners for permission to encroach on part of their land). A tank should not be put where heavy vehicles are likely to pass over it although it must be accessible so that it can be emptied without passing hoses through your cottage. Be clear about the arrangement if a

Figure 63. *Outside toilets make useful storerooms.*

Figures 64, 65, 66 *and* 67. *Laying the drains. Wherever drains change direction there must be access for rods in case of blockage.*

septic tank is to be shared with a neighbour and be equally clear about positioning; we faced this complicated arrangement with one cottage:

> Sewerage. It is intended that a joint septic tank or cesspool will be pro-
> vided by the purchasers to serve both 1 and 2 and 3 Church Cottages,
> local authority permitting, this tank and any soakaways will be situated
> on the ground purchased with number 1 Church Cottages and the
> necessary rights retained for the purchase of numbers 2 and 3. The cost
> of construction and subsequent maintenance of all common parts will
> be borne equally by the purchasers of the two properties. If for any
> reason a joint tank cannot be constructed, then the purchaser of num-
> ber 2 and 3 will construct a tank on their own ground, if permissible,
> with the right to lay soakaways under the ground being sold with num-
> ber 1, and the right to empty it from the land coloured brown. In the
> eventuality of the local authority not allowing a tank within the grounds
> of numbers 2 and 3 the right is reserved for the purchasers of these
> properties to construct it on land being sold with number 1.

Then double the number you first thought of. But better that than a lot of aggravation, even litigation, later.

You may enjoy digging a vegetable patch but if you decide to install a septic tank yourself, *don't* attempt to dig the hole with a spade. You can make better use of your time than spending it behind a shovel; a mechanical digger will remove enough soil for a septic tank in an

Figure 68. *Modern septic tanks work well but involve tearing up gardens.*

hour—it could take you a week. Don't neglect safety with large holes. The sides should either slope or you should shore them up; better still, don't have the hole dug until the septic tank is ready to plonk in, then get enough locals round to complete the job in one day. Holding a Septic Tank Party will at least get you noticed in the village; make a change from Tupperware.

One final point on drainage: a mechanical digger may break into old land drains. You may not be able to prevent the damage but you may get a clue to where they went in case you run into drainage problems later.

Let there be light

If there is no mains electricity connected to your cottage then call at an electricity showroom and ask them to survey the place (preferably before you buy it). The cost of connection to mains electricity will depend on how far cables have to be run and whether additional transformers are needed etc. Could be expensive. If you are very isolated, with no hope of electricity in the area, then you may have to make do with a private generating plant (although this may be offputting to potential buyers when you sell the cottage). I suppose you could consider a windmill or water generator if you are mechanically minded but most people will make do with a normal generating plant. Get one with an automatic start—you don't want to have to keep going out to the thing in the middle of winter. Agricultural engineers may have secondhand ones available.

Having discussed electricity, this seems an appropriate place to discuss wiring and lighting. Remember that misuse of electricity is a major cause of fires in homes and if yours is an unmodernised cottage then it is likely that the wiring needs attention. Don't, repeat *don't*, attempt to lash bits and pieces to an old system. Far better (and cheaper in the long run) to rip it out and start afresh. If you patch instead, you may be patching for evermore with repeated disruption, mess and danger.

If the cottage has not been rewired since the forties, it will almost certainly need attention because the old rubber insulated cable will probably have perished, particularly where it has got hot. Be wary if the wiring looks as if it has been modified by amateurs; it could be dangerous. The Institute of Electrical Engineers has a set of wiring regulations which are recognised as a reasonable standard but the rules are not easy reading—you may need an electrician or builder to interpret them for you. I freely admit that I am scared of electricity and although connecting wires together may not be difficult and, provided you have a tidy, logical mind, you can do your own wiring, I wouldn't recommend it if you have any doubts. Use a skilled electrician. I find it fascinating how they manage to thread wires around the place. Apparently one technique, not much practised now, is to tie a string to a cat and entice it through a restricted area; fine unless there are mice about in which case anything could happen. And did you know what a good electrician will angle cables slightly near to wall light points? Why? Because screws for such fittings are often vertical and if the cable is too, then screws could pierce it.

If you are working directly with an electrician then you must spell out exactly what you want before you can expect to be given a quote. The local electricity board may quote for doing electrical work, but they may be neither cheap nor particularly efficient.

The key to a successful electrical system in a cottage is (here comes that word again) planning. For instance, think through the placing of furniture before planning wiring—a socket won't be much use behind a wardrobe. Bear in mind that well-planned lighting can contribute as much to the atmosphere in a cottage as a careful colour scheme. Sit with a floor plan of the cottage, think about each room, then the relationship of rooms, then mark your electrics on one copy of the plan. There are recognised symbols for sockets and so on, but you won't need to bother, just use a simple code of different colours or whatever—anything provided the electrician can understand you. Having planned everything, now go round the cottage marking with pencil or chalk exactly where you want things placed. We went round one cottage carefully pencilling on the wallpaper where we wanted sockets and switches; a plasterer then helpfully stripped the paper off for us before the electrician had arrived!

If you liaise closely with your electrician he may be able to save money, for instance by suggesting what should, but may not, be obvious, eg wall sockets back-to-back in adjacent rooms, with wires down one wall, will be cheaper than sockets at opposite ends of those rooms.

Stipulate that cables should be 'chased' into the walls, ie hidden. We did not do this in one cottage but found that the wires on show looked so ugly (and off-putting for tenants because it looked dangerous) that we had them chased later. More expense and mess. If cables are run down plastic conduit it will be relatively easy to renew or modify them later.

Even if the budget is tight, try not to skimp on electrics. Have double sockets where possible and two-way switches where important

Figure 69 (Above). *When re-wiring, cables should be supported by extra pieces of wood where possible. Where holes have to be drilled through joists they should be in the centre, well away from any nails which may be driven in for floorboards etc.*

Figure 70 (Below). *From left to right: main switch, cut out, meter, earth leakage circuit breaker (an extra safety feature), slot meter for holiday letting (the collection box is at the bottom right and awaits a padlock) and, on the right hand wall, a fuse box. All fairly typical of what may accumulate in an old cottage and not a pretty sight—but it is a simple matter to make a cover of hardboard.*

(eg for a stair light): both will cost you more if you decide to have them done later. You or your electrician should wire the cottage on a *ring-circuit* with a cable starting from one 30 A fuse and going from socket to socket round the cottage. One 'ring' should serve up to 1,000 square metres of total floor area. All modern plugs, of course, are fused; make sure you put in the right level of fuse for the particular appliance you are using. Things which take a lot of current, such as cookers, should be wired on a separate circuit and heat resistant cable should be used, as it should for immersion heaters.

If possible, have your meter box on an outside wall. The local electricity authority will supply you with a fibreglass box, free of charge, which means that your meters can be read from outside the cottage even if there is no one in when the meterman calls—particularly useful for second homes. Position such boxes on a side wall if possible—they look ugly plonked by a front door.

Now is the time to decide whether you want a slot meter for the electricity. If you want one installed to be read and emptied by the electricity board, apply to your local showroom; they will give you a form and arrange for it to be fitted. If you are letting the cottage and want to install a meter that *you* empty then buy one via *Exchange & Mart* or through your electrician; this type has nothing to do with the electricity board.

The law stipulates lighting standards for places of work so why tolerate poor lighting in a home? Over—rather than under—illuminate the cottage (you can always put lower wattage bulbs in) and pay particular attention to work areas. The cheapest light of all costs nothing and that is 'borrowed' light, for instance gained by putting glass over the door into a bedroom to borrow light for a corridor. A beam in a cottage may make a good place for a lighting track with spotlights but take care not to install a scheme which is too elaborate or ornate—a lighting display fit for Tamla Motown may jar in a two-up two-down. Take care with coloured lighting—it can look totally out of place in a cottage, while if you were once third in your class at a school sports, don't have strobe lighting focused on your trophy—it may look slightly ostentatious. Table lamps with obscene bulging things which constantly change shape? No.

Too much light can give the wrong effect, for instance a harsh light on a picture may throw out glare. Dimmer switches can help a lot in creating the right atmosphere, as can pull-down lights over dining areas (I once played footsy for two hours with an MFI chair).

Light for safety. Dodgy steps or other changes of level should be well lit and a night light for a corridor may be helpful if there are children—a 5-watt lamp will be quite adequate. Fluorescent lamps are nearly three times as efficient as filament lamps of equivalent wattage—don't have them in living rooms (they will look too clinical) but they are ideal for kitchens and bathrooms. If the cottage has a small bathroom, then with a large fluorescent strip light over the mirror you wil probably need no other illumination. You can get strip lights with shaver points built in, but make sure they comply with British Standards. Incidentally, the switch for a bathroom light must either be cord operated for safety or be outside the room. Don't take chances with this or with heaters in bathrooms.

Other points on electrics:

- Take great care with metal fittings; they must be earthed.
- Get a TV aerial and point built in while the wiring is being done; position the set so there will be no direct sunlight on it. A TV aerial in a loft may be less obtrusive than one on a chimney, but if you insulate the loft watch that you don't use materials which insulate the aerial as well.
- Get wall heaters early enough for the electrician to install them at the same time as he does the wiring.
- Plan plenty of sockets in the kitchen.
- Avoid overloading sockets—additional powerpoints are safer than piling adaptors on to one socket.
- Remember sockets in halls and landings for vacuum cleaners.
- Include a loft light in your plans.
- If you are planning electrics for the disabled, the Electricity Council and the Disabled Living Foundation have produced a booklet called *Making Life Easier for Disabled People.*
- If your cottage is in a burglar-prone area, add a timer to your switching system so that lights come on when you are out.
- Don't spoil a well wired house by having telephone wires trailing all over the place—plan the position of the phone with the same care as the rest of the wiring.
- Try to get one coat of paint on walls before electrical fittings are put in place.

Don't just plan lighting for inside the cottage—consider outdoor lighting at the same time to save the disruption of doing it later. If done well it can have a magical effect on the appearance of a cottage. Even if you cannot afford to install outside lighting during the renovation, at least plan where you will take off the power later and build in the appropriate points. The best way to plan outdoor lighting is to walk round the garden with a lamp on a long lead (watching safety of course) to experiment. Go for a soft rather than harsh light and remember a low wattage will be adequate.If you intend holding a barbecue in the garden, then plan appropriate lighting. And, by the way, street lights are intended for streets in towns and may look odd alongside a country cottage. And haven't imitation carriage lamps been done to death?

If you have a thatched cottage with a lot of overhang, the doorstep may get slippery owing to moss or slime—this is encouraged by moisture and darkness—so have proper lighting.

If you made the effort to blend your cottage in with its surroundings, yet the area is spoilt by overhead wires, ask the local electricity board if they will consider putting them underground. They may co-operate. We were faced with new wires running in front of our present house to supply a farm building. We asked politely and the wires were put underground where they pass us; we even receive 10p per year wayleave which comes in quite handy (I don't think you appreciate how we authors struggle).

A final point: when the people from the electricity board come to connect up your wiring, they have a legal duty to make sure that it has a certain level of insulation resistance before they give you a supply. This check may be some comfort to you if you have done your own installation. However, if you have made a mess of it, and they find it faulty, they will not connect and you will be charged for two visits instead of one.

12

Kitchens and Bathrooms

The two rooms in a cottage likely to need most attention are the kitchen and bathroom. In many cottages the kitchen is likely to feature an old white sink with just a cold tap, while there may well be no bathroom at all. Both rooms are vital to the enjoyment of your cottage and, at the risk of becoming a bore, let me stress that the key word, yet again, is planning. The more you plan and the longer you juggle with cut-outs of sink, cooker, and so on, the more likely you are to end up with worthwhile rooms. Incidentally, with both kitchens and bathrooms it saves a lot of mess if you can get at least one coat of paint on the ceilings and walls before units are installed.

Kitchens

Let us take the kitchen first. Your planning will be affected by whether the room is to be just a kitchen or a kitchen-cum-dining room. Once you have established what role the kitchen is to play in your cottage, draw up a 'wants list' of the work surfaces and equipment you need. Consult your wife at this stage of the proceedings because, despite the encroachment of women's lib, she will spend more time in it than you and if you involve her in the planning she won't be able to blame you if it doesn't quite work out. Obviously a cordon bleu will need more work surfaces and utensil space than a two veg and tin-opener cook.

Keep a scrap book or folder of planning ideas torn out of magazines and newspapers. Get hold of catalogues from suppliers of kitchen units; many contain scale drawings which can be cut out and juggled on a floor plan. Most of the manufacturers and some of the monthly house magazines offer planning services. Note that the drawing of your kitchen floor plan must be the most accurate of your cottage because you will have many things to slot in. Allow an inch or two either side of cookers and fridges etc, so that they can be pulled out for

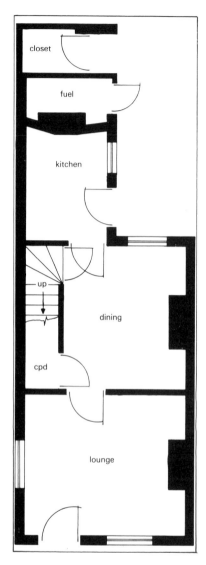

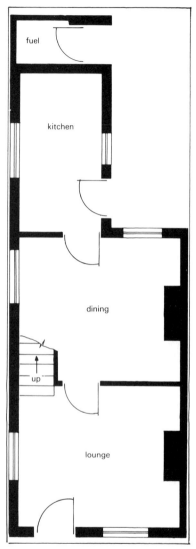

Figure 71. *A typical downstairs layout with an outside closet and fuel store and with cramped stairs leading from a dining room.*

Figure 72. *The closet was retained as a store and the fuel store was incorporated into the kitchen. The stairs were repositioned as shown in* Figures 48 *to* 52.

cleaning. An early decision has to be whether the cooker is to be a free-standing combined unit or a separate oven and hob; if your cottage is for holiday letting or weekend relaxation then go for whatever is easiest to clean. Cookers and fridges are available with left- and right-hand opening doors which may help your planning.

The basic planning of a kitchen is not difficult—you buy food, store it, prepare it,cook it, serve it, eat it, then wash up afterwards so the work surfaces and equipment should be installed to make that cycle as simple as possible. Remember that you will need somewhere to store a vacuum cleaner, brushes, cleaning materials, ironing board and perhaps a pram. If the kitchen has to double as a laundry room then you also need to plan where the washer is to sit.

The key to a successful working kitchen is to have adequate storage. The British Standard lists four categories of food, which require special storage conditions:

1. Dried goods (unopened tinned or bottled food, sugar, tea etc) need to be kept in dry conditions at normal room temperature (+ 12 degrees C or above) in closed cupboards or open shelves—so these present no problems.
2. Semi-perishable foods (bread, preserves, fresh vegetables and fruit) should be kept cool and not too dry in a proper ventilated food store (the old fashioned cool larder with marble shelves is ideal although the modern place for them is likely to be a bread bin).
3. Perishable foods (milk, meat, fish, eggs etc) should be stored in a refrigerator.
4. Frozen foods may be kept in the freezer compartment of an ordinary refrigerator or in a deep freeze.

So although a traditional larder is not necessary nowadays, you will certainly want space for a refrigerator and perhaps a deep freeze (or a fridge/freezer if you want both but are short of space). Incidentally, if you've been reading about self-sufficiency and feel that you should move to a country cottage to grow your own denim and live off natural goats' milk and home-grown vegetables, I have an important piece of advice: lie down until the feeling goes away.

If the cottage has an old Belfast sink on brick pillars then take it out (a local gardener may be glad of it for his bedding plants) and put in a modern one. Although the sink is the key to a kitchen, don't put in one with a triple bowl and double drainers if this leaves the room un-balanced, with inadequate work surface. Despite any old wives' opinions, sinks don't have to be underneath windows (it puzzles me why so often the dining area in a kitchen is away from the window). Stainless steel sinks seem the most durable and you often see second hand ones advertised—they won't shine like a new one but within a few weeks a new one will have lost its gleam too. This is the time to decide if the sink is to house a waste-disposal unit.

Keep in mind that kitchen units are made in various depths—don't make the mistake we did of putting very deep units in a narrow kitchen; there was hardly any room to squeeze between them. Allow 4 ft between opposite work surfaces or units. It is irritating and painful constantly to bump into a work surface; it can be irritating, painful and even dangerous to catch your face on the open door of a wall unit, so take care with positioning. You won't fit a wall unit directly over a cooker will you?

For our cottages (that sounds grandiose so, correction, for our bank's cottages) we have always built up kitchens from various units scrounged off friends, taken off skips or bought at jumbles; we've used the centre piece of a gateleg table to make a thin storage unit and even cut a double wardrobe in two to make a broom cupboard. If you take a similar cheeseparing route, paint all the units the same colour or colours (use white for the basic units and a colour for the doors) and if you have to raise some of the units to bring them up to the height of the others, do so with blocks of wood then paint round the bases in black. If you can afford to homogenise the units with a new set of handles then even Robert Carrier will drool with envy. Several suppliers offer ranges of hinges and fittings to help the rejuvenation of old units and you can get 'carousels' to fit into units to gain access to dead space in corners.

Incidentally, new work surfaces will transform old units and are fairly easy to make. Use a thick chipboard or blockboard (the weight will add stability and give a solid feel to your kitchen—use at least ¾ in thick material), measure carefully, juggle to get the maximum number of work surfaces out of an 8 ft × 4 ft sheet and ask the supplier to cut it for you to save your muscles. Then stick on a laminate (Formica or similar) with the appropriate adhesive. You can buy ready-made 'up-stands' (the strip that goes at the back of a work surface to bridge the gap against the wall) in wood or plastic but, with patience, you should be able to create your own from spare bits of chipboard and Formica. You can buy 'iron-on' trimming for the front edges of work surfaces or, again, cut scrap laminate to fit. If you want a neater job many DIY centres stock ready-made worktops which they will cut to size for you.

If your cottage comes with marble slabs of any sort then consider using them as work surfaces; an undertaker will advise you where to get them cut to size.

Figure 73. *In the cottage shown in the plans in* Figures 71 *and* 72, *the wall was removed between the original kitchen and the coal store to give an enlarged room with a second window. Apart from the sink, all the units were bought at jumbles for under £4 then painted the same colour. Eat your heart out, Terence Conran.*

Having sorted out the kitchen units and work surfaces, take the trouble to get the electrics right; as mentioned earlier, you need plenty of power points. Don't plan a kitchen round an old cooker point if you are having the place rewired because it will be easy to move it to where the cooker should ideally be; where it *should* be is away from through traffic, for safety's sake. For the same reaosn, flexes to kettles or irons should not trail over the hotplate of a cooker. When planning your wiring, consider whether you will need power points for a microwave, cooker hood, extractor fan, waste disposal unit and so on.

Bathrooms

Study the floor plan of your cottage if you have to add a bathroom and, before building on an extension, consider if there is space to squeeze a bathroom or shower into part of a hall or bedroom. With an electric extractor fan fitted, you can have a bathroom in the heart of a cottage without an outside wall or window—we've successfully vented fans into unused chimneys. The easiest way of adding a bathroom will be to convert a small bedroom, although whether you do this or not will depend on your domestic circumstances. If you do convert a bedroom, it will be cheaper to obscure the existing glass in the window with a self-adhesive plastic sheet than to reglaze it.

If you are adding an extension you may be able to place a kitchen and bathroom close together (to save on plumbing) but remember that there must be a ventilated lobby between a WC and living room, unless the WC is off a bedroom and there is another in the cottage. Don't forget to allow space for an airing cupboard.

As with kitchens, send off for manufacturers' brochures for ideas; most suppliers offer planning services, although if you manage to plan your kitchen you should be able to do the bathroom too because there are fewer things to consider.

If your budget is tight, watch the small ads for secondhand bathroom suites for sale—you may be lucky although, despite several attempts, I've never found anything worth buying through this route; if you are more successful, replace any washers before installing the units. And if you buy secondhand, try to match *styles* as well as colours because a modern bath with an old basin and a WC of yet a third age will look odd.

If you decide to buy a new bathroom suite, do shop around. The large discount places will be cheapest, although they may not have the widest choice, and do compare apples and apples when getting quotes—make sure taps, plugs and other fittings are included.

Figures 74 *and* 75. *The small bedroom shown in* Figure 14 *with planks supporting the end wall while that below was removed. An RSJ was installed and the bedroom was then converted into the bathroom shown in* Figure 15.

Figure 76 (Left). *If you convert a bedroom into a bathroom, self-adhesive sheeting as shown on the top left pane will be a lot cheaper to add privacy than reglazing.*

We've had problems when letting holiday cottages with plastic baths because they get scratched, so I feel the extra cost of a steel bath is worthwhile; cast iron ones can be unwieldy for a small cottage. A plastic bath will flex more than a steel one—you need to keep this in mind when you are jointing along the edges because rigid joints may crack. Whether you pay the additional sum for a coloured rather than white suite is entirely up to you. White is the cheapest and you can counter its rather cold effect by the use of warm colours on walls and furnishings.

Position the units in the bathroom for maximum efficiency, comfort and convenience, and do keep drainage runs in mind—the shorter they are, the lower your costs will be. The WC will be the most expensive item to re-position because of drainage runs; provided there is a reasonable slope for the waste runs, the position of basins and baths can be more flexible.

Try not to place the washbasin under a window otherwise there will be no place for a mirror in front of people when shaving and, in your efforts to cram things in, avoid installing a very tiny washbasin because people will soak the floor. You can gain a little extra space for a basin by overhanging it over a bath but don't do this so much that

Figure 77 (Right). *The bath-room on the plan in* Figure 19 *takes shape. The angled wall with the cistern on it has been chipped away to take the corner of the basin (to avoid too much of it over-hanging the bath). The ex-tractor fan feeds into the old chimney. Ideally, rooms like this should receive at least one coat of paint before units are installed—consider the pantomime of painting be-hind those pipes.*

people have to stand 'off-centre' when washing—it feels uncomfort-able. Consider putting a basin in one of the bedrooms to relieve con-gestion in the bathroom; this will be relatively cheap if the wall backs on to the bathroom and the water supply can be taken off easily. If you put a basin into a bedroom, don't make it too big, with a huge worktop, otherwise it will be like sleeping in a public convenience.

If you are very tight for space for a bathroom, bear in mind that you could actually make your own bath to fit an awkward shape (I'm talk-ing about the room, not you) by using tiles and waterproof fixer and grouting. Look around caravan equipment suppliers because they will have very small baths and basins which you may be able to squeeze in. Remember that mirrors (or mirror tiles) will help to make a bathroom seem more spacious. If all else fails, but you have at least 1 x 1 metre available, then build a shower; you really need at least 1.2 metres dif-ference in height between the shower outlet and the draw-off point on your cold water tank for a satisfactory one, although if you fit a booster pump you should be able to fit one anywhere. You may even be able to build a shower cupboard into a living room—if you step out of it as guests arrive it should make any party go with a swing. A shower *must* have an efficient heat control. You may just shriek if the shower suddenly goes cold, it may scald you if it suddenly gets too hot. By the way, a shower with the head on a flexible pipe will be more convenient than a rigidly fixed one.

I guess the only other piece of bathroom equipment to consider is a bidet, for which the local authority may have special regulations. I always feel a bidet is more a conversation piece than anything else, although perhaps it's a strange place to hold a conversation. I'm not convinced that Britain is really Bidet Country. Altogether now, 'Rule Britannia . . .'

Nor is a sauna likely to be part of your cottage planning, although these too have their advocates. I have taken saunas in Finland and thoroughly enjoyed them but I can never see them taking hold in Britain. Still, if you think that a big blonde beating your buttocks with a birch bough will prolong your active life . . . build in a sauna. By the way, my guide to saunas says 'the wooden shack is nice for contemplation, and courtesy demands that each should offer to wash the sauna companion's back'. My pleasure (would you mind turning over the page?).

Having finished all your bathroom planning, pause and consider safety. You will, of course, have planned the electrics properly for any shaver point as well as heating and lighting, but if you have converted a ramshackle old cottage, are any steps into the bathroom safe? If not, make them so while if you add a bathroom cabinet get one with a childproof catch.

Finally, to save people having to sing as they sit in solitude, put a bolt on the bathroom door, preferably one which can be opened from outside in an emergency.

Plumbing

Kitchens and bathrooms have been grouped together in this chapter because they have one thing in common—they need plumbing. If you need to find a plumber, remember that there are more cowboys in this trade than most other sections of building, so try the word-of-mouth method or consult a library or water authority for the *Business Directory of Plumbers* issued by the Institute of Plumbing. Take the trouble to brief a plumber properly and if you want unusual taps or fittings, tell him in good time for him to order them.

Although you may be too cautious to attempt your own house wiring, you could feel brave enough to have a go at plumbing—if you get wiring wrong you can electrocute yourself, if your plumbing is sloppy you will just get soaked. Modern fittings are simple to use if you follow

Figure 78. *A ready assembled water system like this may be dearer than one built up on site but will be simpler and quicker to install. Paint the walls before the unit goes in.*

manufacturers' instructions carefully, but resist the temptation to graft new bits of piping on to an old system—it will be cheaper in the long run to rip the old plumbing out and start afresh. Before you do anything, consult your local water authority because the DIY man is subject to the same bylaws, regulations and controls as the professional plumber. Everything connected to the water supply—taps, ballvalves, pipes, washing appliances—has to comply with the Water Bylaws made and enforced by water undertakings for 'preventing waste, undue consumption, misuse or contamination of water supplied by them'. It is illegal to use fittings which do not conform to the Water Bylaws; most water undertakings accept fittings and materials which have been tested and accepted by the National Water Council. Before carrying out any alterations to water fittings, or to an existing supply, seven days' notice must be given to the water undertaking. Well, that's the theory anyway.

Other points to keep in mind about plumbing:

- Keep pipe runs short to reduce costs and to prevent semi-stagnant water lingering for long periods.
- Avoid dips in pipe runs—one gave us a burst pipe where water lay in a valley when we blissfully thought we had drained the system.
- Think ahead. If you plan to add an extra wash basin later, build in the appropriate take-off point from the start.
- Plastic piping will not give you an electrical earth.
- If your cottage has no water system, a prefabricated unit will be a lot more convenient than assembling one from scratch but it may be more expensive.
- Paint an airing cupboard before the hot water cylinder goes in—otherwise you will never get behind it.
- Put an insulating jacket round the hot water cylinder. To put water heating into perspective, it is likely to take about a quarter of your total energy costs.
- Using old taps? Replace the washers because a dripping tap will stain a bath or basin and may block a waste pipe in winter.
- If your cottage has an old galvanised cold water storage tank which is leaking, replace it with a plastic one (which can be squeezed through a trap door). Do put a lid on it, weighted down, to stop animals getting in. Mice are just about the right size to block pipes and, forgive me if you are eating, a friend even had maggots come through a tap from a rotting rat.
- If you are adding a water storage tank in a loft, position it over a warm room so that it won't freeze in winter; tuck it out of the way if you are planning to add a room in the loft later. In an old cottage place the tank near the brick walls or a chimney stack to take the load—old joists are often too small to take additional loading. Put the tank close to the bearing ends of the joists.
- It is worth replacing the ball valve if you retain a very old WC—newer types are much quieter. If you are switching from a well to mains water supply you will have to modify things in order to cope with the change from low to high pressure.
- Consider building in a water softener if you live in a very hard water area.
- Sluggish waste pipes are inconvenient so clean them out every so often.
- Know where your stop taps are!

Finally, after the plumbing is completed in your cottage, you may hear horrible noises called 'hammering' (which must be particularly distressing if you are a stockbroker). Try turning down the stop tap to reduce the pressure. If this doesn't stop the noise, check the pipes—a length may be vibrating because it isn't fixed firmly. Finally, check the taps because the sound may be caused by washers jumping up and down.

It's all go, isn't it?

13

Heating

Having renovated your cottage you will want to keep it warm and pleasant to live in; you will certainly want enough heat to protect its fabric.

Ideally, living rooms should have a temperature around 20 degrees C (68 degrees F); kitchens get heat from cookers etc, so can be targeted lower (say, 17 degrees C, 63 degrees F) while bedrooms need only 16 degrees C (61 degrees F). Put these figures up if the cottage is to be used by elderly people and, above all, allow for plenty of heat in a bathroom where, unless you have unusual ablution habits, you will be minus some or all of your clothes.

Actually, in any debate on energy resources, we should perhaps keep in mind that wearing more clothes is the cheapest way of heating. Bring back layers of thick flannel underwear (which would have the double advantage of curbing the birth rate).

In planning the heating of your cottage take care that you don't create a whole new set of problems. Old houses were usually well ventilated (in other words, draughty) with hardly any heating and as a result they had few condensation problems. The dreaded condensation occurs when warm moist air hits a cold surface—the air is cooled, it is less able to hold moisture, and the excess moisture forms on cold surfaces (such as windows) as droplets of water. The water then runs down the window, which is why you get black mould along the bottom of window panes. There may be few condensation problems in a cottage until you improve it by sealing up chimneys, adding a hot water supply, subdividing large airy rooms into little boxes, putting in central heating and making it draught-proof. You need a balanced approach to heating because turning your cottage into an airtight heated box may create problems—not least of which could be that you will suffocate.

Rising costs must force people into a more common-sense

approach to heating; as an example, boiling a kettle is cheaper than running gallons of hot water through a system to the kitchen tap—it's not the water you use that wastes money, but the gallon which stays in the pipes and cools.

Similarly, keep in mind things to avoid condensation: have a kettle with a cut-off so that it is not left steaming away merrily in a kitchen; put lids on saucepans; run cold water into a bath before adding hot, and so on. Extractor fans will help although they may extract heat from a room too. A small point with ventilators: noisy ones can be very irritating. For bathrooms you can get fans that come on automatically with light switches and stay on for some minutes after the light is turned off. Tiny window ventilators powered by the breeze, which go round and round like kids' windmills, are little use.

If your cottage is only used in the summer then instead of the horrific cost of heating it during the winter, consider a different approach and keep it dry by installing a dehumidifier. This operates on the refrigeration principle and draws air into a dryer; the air then passes over a radiator coil which is constantly maintained at a temperature around freezing point. One we hired, then bought later, is

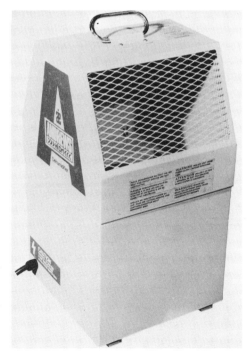

Figure 79. *A dehumidifier like this may be cheaper and simpler than heating to keep a cottage dry during winter months. Consider hiring one for a season to try it before buying.*

capable of pulling 3 gallons of water out of the air every 24 hours. Don't put one by an open window—your high electricity bill will be high because you are trying to dry out Great Britain.

If you decide that you must have heating then first establish whether you want full or background heating. The former is better because in very cold weather it will be capable of making the whole cottage warm. Background heating hasn't much to commend it—you will find yourself endlessly adding extra electric fires and so on; best to get the system right from the start. If you can't afford a fullblown system at this stage at least install a boiler big enough for the whole cottage with just a few radiators, coupling up others later. Adding new central heating equipment to an old-fashioned decrepit system may not be successful; it will probably be cheaper, and certainly more practical, to rip out the old stuff and start afresh.

Try to have a flexible heating system, this particularly applies with a place which you only visit at weekends or for holidays because you will need to get heat moving quickly. I guess with the micro-chip revolution it should be possible to telephone a cottage and 'tell' the heating to switch itself on.

A few points to bear in mind when considering heating:

- You are likely to be living with radiators for a long time so choose ones to blend with your cottage. Remember that two single panel radiators, if you have the wall space for them, will put out more heat than a double panelled one of the same size.
- Theory has it that radiators should go under windows, but I am not convinced; placing one on a wall may be as effective. Don't cover a radiator with long curtains down to the floor otherwise all you will be doing is heating the window behind them.
- Skirting radiators are unobtrusive but you may not have enough wall space for them to heat a cottage adequately.
- For rapid warm up, a convector heater with a variable speed fan, working exactly like a car heater, is effective. Choose one which is quiet.
- It is possible to bury central heating pipes in concrete floors but as I have had to have a floor dug up because of a leaking joint, I would not recommend it. In fact some water authorities may not allow you to buy pipes anyway and running them in the open will give you a little extra heat.
- It will often be convenient to drop pipes downwards from the floor above. In this case try to tuck them into a corner of a room and paint them the same colour as surrounding walls.

- A boiler must have an adequate air supply, which may mean putting air vents near to it.
- Fit control units which will let you programme the heating to suit your particular requirements.
- Remember that warmth alone won't make you comfortable because unless air is moving around, a room will get stuffy and you may have condensation. Keep this in mind when insulating and draught proofing.

Ever noticed how high chimney stacks are on old houses? They were not designed just to look pretty, they were built when people were burning wood and had to contend with down draught. If you have converted an old cottage, a chimney which has worked perfectly well through the centuries may not necessarily suit your new central heating system and, although you can study local wind patterns, even the cleverest installer may not be able to forecast how well a chimney will work. You may have to have your chimney/s lined. If your boiler is fired by oil or gas you can have a stainless steel lining inserted in an existing chimney, connected to a length of flue pipe from the boiler at one end and to the chimney pot at the other. If the space between this lining and the chimney is filled with insulating material it will help to keep the temperature up and the condensation down. (Stainless steel linings are not effective with solid fuel.)

Having given thought to your heating system, you now have to decide how to install it. If you have conquered the mysteries of plumbing or done your own wiring then you should be able to tackle central heating. It is only an extension of plumbing, after all, and modern fittings are a great help. If you take this route, most of the DIY magazines as well as *Exchange & Mart* have advertisements from equipment suppliers to the home installer and most offer catalogues and planning advice. Mind, it is still worth studying the subject in some detail and working out your own radiator requirements etc as a cross-check.

If you decide to have the work done professionally and see the phrase 'approved installer', ask 'approved by whom?'; it may simply be by the people whose goods the installer uses and such an installer may only be competent with the use of one particular type of fuel.

The recognised organisation representing the trade is the Heating and Ventilating Contractors Association. Their members offer a guarantee scheme covering materials and workmanship for 12 months but, more important, the scheme is backed by the Association who should honour the guarantee even if your installer goes broke while you are still trying to get the boiler to fire. Although you should go for a member of the HVCA if possible, still the safest way of finding some-one is through friends; an installer operating in the locality with a local reputation to protect is likely to be the safest choice.

The most difficult decision over heating is to decide what fuel and system to use. For simplicity I suppose we can dismiss warm air systems here and now (whatever the fuel used) because they are really better for new houses where the ducting can be built in from scratch than for cottages. I think the Romans had the earliest form of warm air heating when they lit a fire in the basement then let heat travel up between the walls of a house and out at the top; mind you they did have slaves to do all the work.

Fuel suppliers advertise heavily, so you will have to plough your way through the blandishments of all the vested interests. If yours is an isolated cottage, you need to consider the availability of supply.

- Will an oil tanker be able to get down your lane and reach your tank?
- Will people be prepared to deliver at all? If you only have a small tank and live in an out of the way place, you may have to pay a surcharge.
- Is there any gas in the village?
- Will your existing chimney suit one sort of fuel and not another?
- Above all, what about cost? You will probably be able to get a loan for a central heating installation particularly if you use one of the major companies. Calculate carefully before switching from one fuel to another—it could take forever to save enough on running costs to pay for the installation.

Now let us consider the various fuels in a little more detail.

Solid fuel

Psychologically nothing beats a coal fire. Just think of the muffins toasting . . . your warm hands . . . your glowing face . . . your cosy feet . . . your freezing back.

Various back boilers are available to fit into existing fireplaces which will supply a central heating system but they need attention several times a day and are only suitable for relatively small installations. It is now possible to link an open fire room heater with a back boiler to an oil or gas fired central heating system so that it takes over when the fire is lit (either to heat the water or provide a full heating system).

Anyone who has an Aga cooker appears to rave about it while modern free-standing stoves look elegant if you get them to blend with the cottage; some may bring back service memories for older readers. If you have a chimney added on an outside wall for a coal fire, it is worth having an outside access panel so that you can remove ashes and clean the fire without carrying them through the cottage.

If you settle for a coal fire, and are sitting comfortably, here is a cautionary tale. A friend owned a 250-year-old cottage and installed a solid fuel boiler in an existing fireplace to heat seven radiators as well as domestic hot water. The cottage was typical of its age, the inside of the chimney breast was enormous and as a result the updraught was poor. The owner made the mistake of ordering a small anthracite fuel and the combination of poor draught and small fuel resulted in a slow burning fire. On a still, damp day, there was an explosion in the top of the chimney because unburned gases had accumulated inside the chimney stack and ignited, causing several hundred pounds' worth of damage. An investigation by an inspector from the Solid Fuel

Advisory Service showed that the explosion was caused by an accumulation of factors:

1. The size of the chimney breast which at the time housed a large cooking range. The inspector suggested fitting a special pipe over the top of the boiler to improve the updraught.
2. The chimney pot had a large cowl fitted over it which further reduced the airflow; this was left off when the chimney stack was rebuilt.
3. The size of the fuel. The inspector suggested that much larger fuel be used.

With all those changes that particular cottage now has a beautiful, bright fire. But the moral is, if in doubt, consult the appropriate authorities for advice. There is one other moral: be adequately insured. My friend wasn't—his cottage was insured for £15,000 but the insurers found its current worth to be £22,000 and only paid 15/22 of the repair bill.

Solid fuel heating is not ideal for weekend cottages where you need to be able to switch on a system then forget it. If you do opt for solid fuel, buy the largest bunker you can comfortably house in your garden because prices may be lower for bulk deliveries. Experts (I once saw an expert defined as anyone more than 200 miles from home) reckon that there is enough coal left to last for 300 years so this could be the fuel for you if you are thinking of settling down.

Wood stoves

Wood stoves are quite the in things and you may find the smell of burning wood attractive, while ash makes a useful fertiliser. Wood stoves are not as primitive as they sound, you can get domestic hot water heated by one and have cooking plates on top. So if you think you can lay your hands on 50lb or so of seasoned hardwood a day, a wood burning stove may be your answer. If nothing else, felling all that timber will keep you fit. Let wood dry out as much as possible before burning it; logs which have been cut and dry stored for a year are the best, although ash burns well even if it has only recently been cut. Hawthorn, larch and oak are good but avoid wood with a lot of resin like pine and fir.

Where a fire is log-fuelled the chimney flue must be fairly large for smoke to escape. Preferably for a wood stove your chimney should be fitted with a clay flue liner or a stainless steel flue as previously mentioned. Do bear in mind that wood is *not* a smokeless fuel so you could be breaking the law if the cottage is in a smoke control area.

Figure 81. *These oil-filled electric radiators may be neat and unobtrusive but they are expensive to run.*

Electricity

Heating by electricity is easy to install with little disruption. Maintenance is minimal and there is no need for any fuel store but electricity produces a very dry heat and it is not cheap to run. With one unit of electricity you can brown 70 slices of toast in a toaster or (even more useless information) open over 6,000 cans in an electric can-opener but you can only operate a 2 kW heater for half an hour. Relying on electric fires for heating is one of the most expensive ways known to man, although there is just one advantage if you are furnishing a cottage on the cheap—electric fires rarely fetch more than a pound or two at auctions.

You can use electricity for underfloor or ceiling heating but neither is likely to be suitable for an old cottage; night storage heaters may be though. These take in their heat load during off-peak and therefore cheaper periods and discharge it over the following day. This means that to use them effectively you need some talent as a weather forecaster—a postgraduate qualification in meteorology would do nicely. Some of them have a fan to push out the heat which helps if you want a quick warm up for a room. Storage heaters are bulky and keep in mind that their kW rating does not represent the amount of heat put into the room but only the amount of heat put into storage. Like electric fires, storage heaters can be very cheap if bought through classified small ads, as can electrically powered oil-filled radiators.

Oil

Here I must declare an interest: I have had four oil-fired central heating systems put into various places and been satisfied with all of them.

One problem with oil if you only have a small garden may be finding space for a storage tank. If neighbours are restoring cottages at the same time as you, consider a larger tank somewhere with separate metering which would help you to buy oil cheaper and ensure deliveries. Various types of boilers are available of all shapes and sizes so you should readily find a system to suit your cottage. Keep the sound level in mind when choosing a boiler.

Paraffin heaters? Well, the problem of keeping wicks trimmed has always been beyond my embroidery skills and in addition, every pint of paraffin burned by a heater produces a pint of water, so if you are not careful you can have condensation problems. There may be a smell with a paraffin heater but nevertheless one may be convenient to augment a heating system.

Gas

If there is no gas in the vicinity of your cottage then you can move on to the next section. If you do have gas available then here is some more relatively useless information: one therm of gas will run a fridge for seven days but a gas fire for only five hours on high setting. If you go for gas, you must have the system properly installed by a reputable company. Once installed, gas appliances should be checked at least once a year and remember that to burn safely and efficiently gas needs a supply of fresh air. This may come into the room from outside the house or from a well ventilated adjoining room. Many gas appliances must have a chimney or flue so that fumes are taken directly out of the house. If this gets blocked or damaged, dangerous fumes can be forced back into a room. So flues must work properly and be clear of obstructions.

The most modern way for many gas appliances to breathe in and out is by a system known as a 'balanced flue'. Appliances using this system are fixed to any convenient wall through which a small hole can be made directly to the outside of the house. The appliance is fully sealed from the room, fresh air is drawn in directly from the outside through one part of the system, while fumes are discharged through another. Only appliances of this type may now be fitted in bathrooms. Above all know how to turn off your mains gas supply—the tap will usually be near to the meter.

Gas can provide sound central heating and there is a run on gas at the moment because of its cheapness (perhaps I should add that 'cheapness' is a relative term because *all* heating is expensive). For a small cottage, a combined unit of gas fire-cum-boiler built into the hearth space (again with a lined chimney) may be suitable although these are only really good in a small installation.

You should have gas fires checked regularly; British Gas will carry out a check on one for a relatively small sum, checking for leaks etc. It's worth having a fire checked if you have bought it secondhand.

If you like gas and are moving to a cottage without it, then you could use bottled gas instead. It is claimed to be as powerful and reliable as mains gas (but will be more expensive) and it is clean, non-poisonous and you can run fridges, cookers, heaters etc off it; portable heaters seem particularly popular with cottage owners because they are so convenient.

Solar heating

This is unlikely to be of much use for an old cottage because a house should be designed from the start with solar heating in mind. Panels on the roof may help a little if you have to re-roof anyway but they could look odd and it may take a long time to get your money back. In my view, unless you are very knowledgeable about the subject I think it is too early to be using solar heating for an old cottage. Let others experiment first.

If you think about it, a domestic central heating system is really not much different from the 'central heating' in a car. In fact, future heating systems will get even closer to cars because it is now possible for a heat pump, using natural gas or liquefied petroleum gas (LPG), to recycle waste hot water from, for instance, baths, showers and kitchens, so that it operates a central heating system. So maybe in the future instead of an oil or gas-fired boiler you will have a converted car engine ticking over with its own pump (which will mean you won't need electricity). It will have low pollution, be low on noise and it won't be using a scarce energy source because most oil-producing countries have surpluses of natural gas and LPG which is either flared-off or pumped back into wells. An engine from a small family car would be capable of heating at least half a dozen typical small cottages so, if you are an innovator and your cottage is in a row and you can persuade your neighbours to co-operate, this could be a more productive field to explore than solar heating. But only if you are an innovator.

If your chosen system of central heating has a boiler, try to be present when it is fired up for the first time. While the fitter is there, get him to explain all the various taps and pipes; colour code them and mark up a plan with his help.

Remember that central heating will work best if it is maintained properly; most installers offer maintenance and/or insurance schemes.

Insulation

Having installed a heating system in your cottage the most crucial thing is to keep any heat *in*. I know Scandinavia is a lot colder than Britain but we are still way behind them in such things as glazing and insulation in general; Scandinavians think nothing of having triple glazing and 6 in insulation over a roof and in external walls. Leaving them listening to Sibelius, insulating a loft could cut heat loss through your ceiling by around 80 per cent. You will waste a lot of heat if a roof is not felted under the tiles, so have this done if the tiles have to come off, while the best time to do roof insulation may also be when the tiles are off or you have scaffolding up.

Use the thickest loft insulation you can afford and fit it yourself—it is one of the easier DIY jobs. Measure the loft and buy all the material at once and do shop around; your best bet might be through one of the discount stores.

Before you start, remove the mice, skeletons, old bricks and newspapers which seem to accumulate in lofts. Check the wiring because it could be dangerous to cover up with insulation material any which is faulty. Lay a board across the joists or else you may come through the ceiling (I have) and take the insulation material up into the loft unopened, it is much easier to handle this way as it expands when the wrapping is off. Start laying at the eaves but leave gaps for ventilation to avoid condensation.

Insulate the cold water storage tank and cover it to stop creepy crawlies getting in but don't put insulation under the tank—you want heat rising from below to reach it. Don't be tempted to economise by using old blankets and flannel underwear as insulation—they retain water and attract mice.

Lag the hot water cylinder with a jacket conforming to British stan-

Figure 82. *A sure sign that an old cottage is draughty! When removing a splendid old rod like this, don't scrap it but tie all the fittings together so that it is complete if you need to reuse it.*

dard BS 5615: 1978; it will quickly pay for itself. Don't cover the cap or cable of an immersion heater. Put insulation material over pipe runs and if you have a very long pipe run to a particular point, say a basin, consider an electric water heater there to avoid running off lots of water every time you wash.

It all sounds laborious and expensive, but cheer up because under the government's House Insulation Scheme you can get two-thirds of the cost of materials and work (the elderly can get even more) up to a certain limit which is increased from time to time.

Don't be afraid to apply for a grant (over three-quarters of a million have done so), you only have to fill in a simple form available from your local council. You will have to use materials approved by the council and you must get permission before you start. Get hold of the leaflet 'Save Money on Loft Insulation' and the booklet 'All about Loft, Tank and Pipe Insulation' which spell out all the details. You won't get a grant to insulate a loft if you already have any insulation in it, nor will you get a grant if the loft is only immediately above rooms used for storage or for business—it must be immediately above living accommodation. If you have no way into your loft, you can be paid a grant on the cost of making one, but only for cutting a temporary hole and for making good afterwards; you cannot be paid for making a permanent hatch! Finally, you will only get a grant if you use the insulation products on your council's approved list. You must put in at least the thickness of loft insulation stipulated—you can put in more but the grant will be calculated on the basis of the required thickness only. Don't forget that to claim your grant you must be able to produce receipts for all materials and services you have paid for. If the insulation work is part of a larger job you should ensure that it is shown separately.

If your cottage dates before the 1920s, it is unlikely that you will be able to make use of cavity wall insulation but, if you can, do choose an installer on the Agrement Board List of Approved People and above all get a very clear-cut guarantee. Like all new ideas cavity wall insulation has attracted crooks. Care.

If you have to replaster an external wall, consider using a plasterboard with an insulating material already fixed to it. As well as adding insulation, you will improve moisture resistance. Such boards are available in standard sizes and are as easy to fix for the DIY man as normal plasterboard.

Double glazing windows is something which most people should be able to do themselves. Some experts consider double glazing overrated as a heat saver but it certainly helps condensation in places like bathrooms. Some house insurance companies will consider a lower premium because of better security—presumably the lazy thief can't be bothered to cut through two layers of glass. It may take years to recoup the cost of a professionally fitted double glazing system but several DIY schemes are available; one great advantage is that you can start with one window and do others as you have the time and money.

Draught excluders

Draught excluders are many and varied and even easier to fit than double glazing. Measure the whole cottage before you buy any excluder, then test a small sample of the particular make you fancy. Once you are satisfied that it suits your purpose, buy the rest in bulk, not in single door or single window packs, then *read the instructions*. If there are unused keyholes in your cottage then block them up or put escutcheon plates over them to stop the wind whistling through.

An ordinary open fire pulls about 8,500 cubic feet of air an hour from the room it is in—the air has to be replaced so don't make a room totally air tight or else it will be dangerous. A gap across the top of a door will let air in without causing uncomfortable draughts.

Figures 83 *and* 84. *An open porch like this may offer little protection. Panelling the sides, as here, will help; the hammering has left tiles needing attention. Note the new downpipe.*

So far we have considered insulating against cold and draughts but if noise is a problem in your cottage there is a free DOE pamphlet 'Insulation against Traffic Noise' which spells out your rights under the noise insulation regulations. If a new road comes by you or 747s start landing on your greenhouse, you may get help with double glazed windows, insulated doors etc.

A final thought on insulation. Don't spend a fortune on something in a tempting pack in the DIY shop if it is going to take a lifetime to recoup your investment.

14

Decorating and Furnishing

Decorating is well within most people's ability but don't under-estimate the effort or time it will take. If you make a hurried, slapdash job of this stage of the renovation (perhaps because you are getting fed up with the whole process) you will mar all your other work and undermine the value of your cottage.

First, a few general points for the DIY decorater:

- If your cottage comes with old lino (or carpets), take it up to check for rot or woodworm, then put it back to catch paint splashes. Throw it away when the job is finished.
- Leave off new skirting boards and architraves (the trimmings around doorways) until you have painted ceilings and walls.
- Choose brushes and other equipment with care. You can do most painting jobs, apart from large walls and ceilings, with 1 in, 2 in and 3 in brushes. Received wisdom is to buy the best but if you are an untidy worker who forgets to clean brushes, buy cheaper ones and replace them when they get rock hard. Paint rollers are quicker than brushes but I've never liked them; it always seems easier to work paint into a surface with a brush. Others swear by sheepskin pads.
- Buy sufficient paint. Apart from wasting time having to go for more tins if you run out, you could get a colour mis-match.
- If your decorating involves several different gloss colours, save money by choosing colours which use a common undercoat.
- Start by tidying up one room, then use it as a base for your equipment.
- Try to clear a room completely before starting on it. At the very least put furniture in the middle of the room and cover it.
- Have plenty of rags to hand and, to repeat the advice in an earlier chapter, wear old clothes. Forget the ads showing people

decorating in spotless clothes—yours *will* get spotted; I've found a diving suit most appropriate. A plastic carrier bag will help keep your hair clean; to add a touch of class, I use one from Harrods (I once bought a loaf there).

- Keep safety in mind when painting. A ladder should be 2 or 3 ft taller than the highest point you need to reach and, when in position, should be about 1 ft from the wall for every 4 ft of ladder height.
- To avoid elongating your arms, buy or make a simple hook to hang paint tins on to a ladder rung.
- *Read the instructions on tins!*

Exterior work

Protect the outside of your cottage first. Get the dizzy jobs out of the way at the start by painting woodwork around the roof area; if the thought scares you, then use a professional for this if you can afford it. Use binoculars to check his work.

Next, tackle the walls. If there is evidence of damp penetrating through brickwork, make good the pointing, replace badly damaged bricks then brush or spray on a silicon waterproofer. If you are colour-washing rendered outside walls, do choose colours with care; the shade you choose may even be influenced by the area of the country your cottage is in—consider how splendid pink cottages look in Suffolk against the cornfields—but try not to pick a colour which clashes with neighbouring properties. I recommend that you play safe and use a recognised brand of paint rather than some new wonder product guaranteed to last for generations.

Paint from the top of the cottage downwards but don't carry a light colour right down to the ground because it will get dirty too quickly; instead, finish with a foot or so of dark paint. Put something on surrounding paths to catch your drips. If your cottage has an oddball chimney that is out of proportion it will be less obtrusive if painted the same colour as the walls.

If you are fortunate enough to have decorative old oak timber on your cottage and it is unpainted, leave it thus because oak in its natural state will last for years. Painting may trap damp and accelerate rot.

Any galvanised ironwork is best left to weather until it becomes dull before it is painted. If you can't wait that long then rub it down with a medium grade abrasive paper and wipe it over with a white spirit before painting. Scrape or wirebrush new metalwork to remove rust and loose material, then apply a primer. Don't leave new metalwork exposed for long, particularly if you have it sandblasted or steam treated, otherwise it will rust very quickly. Aluminium should be rubbed down with a fine abrasive paper then cleaned before being painted with primer.

Incidentally, use gloss paint on any outside brick windowsills—textured wall finishes won't stand the dirt.

Don't paint plastic guttering otherwise you will have to maintain it for evermore. Mask guttering with a piece of cardboard when decorating walls behind it so that it doesn't get splashed.

Obviously, don't paint outside if it looks as if it is about to rain or if it is windy or there are insects swarming around. Follow the sun when painting and don't paint in direct sunlight because not only will it make it difficult to see which part is painted, it can also lead to blistering as the paint dries. The brightness could even make you giddy enough to fall off a ladder too. Take your time when painting the outside of your cottage, do watch the safety angle and, if it is any consolation, remember that paint properly applied should last at least five years.

Internal decoration

Now let us move inside the cottage, and doing so reminds me that early purchases should include a footscraper and doormat, particularly if paths have not been laid. The first thing to do inside is to protect new woodwork, so, if you had new stairs put in, cover the treads with cardboard so that they don't get grubby before you paint or varnish them. Next, remember that this is the best time to get access to everywhere so, if you have time, it is worth stripping the cottage back to the bare walls. Start by removing old wallpaper; if it has been on a cottage for years it should be stripped off to prepare a firm surface for new paper or paint. Either use a steam stripper or soak the paper with a solution of warm water and either washing up liquid or a proprietary stripper then, when the paper is soaked through, scrape it off with a stripping knife. It won't always be that easy, of course, because some wallpaper can be a nightmare to shift; if so, score it with a knife or attack it with a strong wire brush before you soak it so that the water can penetrate. If it is a vinyl wall covering, peel away the patterned surface then soak the backing paper exactly as normal wallpaper. You will, of course, get the family to help you in all this won't you? Get younger children to work round the bottom of a room with older offspring tackling the middle section. Stop short of sending them up chimneys though—vacuum sweeping methods make far less mess.

If the inside walls of your cottage are not wallpapered but painted then old flaking paint must be removed before decorating. If the paint is old distemper and it is hard and not powdery then you may get away with emulsion on top of it but the real test is to wet the end of a finger and rub it on the wall. If the paint comes off this means that it is a water soluble distemper or whitewash. It means you have trouble because this *must* be totally removed. If you paint over it with any modern paint it will just flake off, looking as if someone has punched a hole through from inside the wall. All the old paint just has to come off by scraping and washing (keep changing the water). Of all the jobs involved in renovating an old cottage I reckon this is the worst. At times the shock of scraping and painting a wall then finding several patches bursting out a day or two later has nearly caused us to pack it all in. If you can afford to have someone do the job for you then for heaven's sake do so.

One builder keeps telling us we must put a sealer or barrier paint on even after thoroughly scraping off whitewash but we haven't done so and we've had no problems. You *will* need a sealer if you have brown stains showing on plaster; you may find ordinary white undercoat effective for small patches. The stains are usually caused by damp penetration and may be worst on chimneys.

On a happier note, walls which have recently been painted with either an oil paint or emulsion really only need a wash down with a weak, warm detergent to remove dirt and deposits. Rinse off with clean water afterwards then let the surface dry thoroughly before repainting.

Having made the effort to remove wallpaper and old paint, don't skimp on the preparation of the walls beneath. It says on paint tins that surfaces should be 'sound, clean and dry' so make them so. Start by removing any old nails before you plaster or paint, otherwise they will rust then show through. Any mould will usually be caused by dampness, condensation, bad ventilation or just lack of light. Treat affected areas with appropriate fungicide.

Repairing routine damage to plaster on walls should be well within the reach of a modest DIY man (or woman, I hasten to add), although a large damaged area of wall may need a professional plasterer. You must make good any cracks and holes before putting new wallpaper on, particularly if this is thin, because holes and cracks will show. Conversely, lumps on walls should be sanded or scraped level before painting or wallpapering. If there are lots of tiny holes, perhaps where

Christmas cards have been pinned up over the years, do take the trouble to fill them—don't rely on paint to do so. If you use one of the heavily advertised fillers, buy it in sizeable bags if you have plenty of work—they are much cheaper than cartons. Ordinary plaster will do just as well and will be even cheaper. Try to learn the knack of mixing whatever plaster you use—I swing wildly from too much water to too much plaster and waste a lot of time. You really need to work out that so many yoghurt cartons of plaster mixed with so many of water will give you the correct mix. Wet the surface to be plastered by flicking clean water at it with a brush—don't worry about splashing it about—

Figure 85. *Don't be too eager to throw old material into a skip. Old bricks from the derelict outhouses shown in* Figure 31 *were used to make a new grate and block up an archway. Marks on the walls are sealer to stop old distemper breaking through new emulsion.*

then wipe the wet brush over your new plaster to smooth it. All quite satisfying really. Any areas of loose or poor plasterwork should be removed and the edges cut back to sound plaster; if you don't do this new plaster will simply crumble off along with the next batch of old to give way. Brush away all dust and debris when you have hacked the plaster away and fill large holes in stages, allowing each layer to dry before applying the next; plug large holes with bricks.

By the way, professional plasterers seem to work best with Radio 1 blaring out at full blast; perhaps the din frightens the plaster into setting.

Still on the subject of preparation, stripping old gloss paint off woodwork is a nuisance but if the paint in your cottage is bad then it is worth doing this job so that you start afresh with a good surface. Use a hot air stripper, a liquid paint remover or, more traditionally, a blowlamp—use the latter with care because you are literally playing with fire. Above all, keep the blowlamp flame moving about so that you lift the paint without burning the woodwork. Take the paint off as it starts to blister and don't let the flame play too long on window panes or you may crack the glass. If using chemical paint removers, wear rubber gloves and old clothes and *read the instructions* on the container. Allow a stripper to work before you start scraping off paint; if the paint is very thick you may need more than one application.

Whichever way you strip (that was charming, madam: you can put your clothes back on now) clean the surface afterwards with white spirit, sand it down and dust it off, and there you are, ready to repaint. If you don't want to go to the trouble of stripping off paint completely (and avoid it if you can) then old gloss surfaces should be rubbed down with an abrasive paper to provide a key for the new coat. Don't use too coarse an abrasive as this will cause scratches to show through. Remember that cracks and open joints in new wood can be made good with putty or wood filler; open grain scratches should be filled with a fine plaster then smoothed down before being primed.

Scheming

Hopefully, you now have a cottage which is structurally sound, all the walls have been stripped and the old gloss paint has been removed or sanded. Time to decorate? Yes, but pause before you flail about with a brush. Give some thought to the decoration because the colour schemes you choose must be in harmony with your lifestyle and with your particular cottage. When planning the schemes, consider what items you already have: carpets, curtains etc, but remember it will be a false economy to base a room's colour scheme on a pair of curtains which are really ready for a jumble sale.

Plod around showhouses to pinch ideas and remember that many of the glossy monthly magazines offer room planning services (for a fee). I've used one of these a couple of times and the replies have been fairly conventional but nonetheless helpful. It would be impertinent of me to tell you what colours to use but, without prejudice or malice aforethought, here are a few general points:

- If yours is a small cottage remember that the fewer changes in colour and pattern the greater the harmony and the bigger the place will look.
- Big, bold wallpaper patterns may make a room look tense and small.
- Avoid gimmicks. A hunt in full cry painted over a fireplace may look clever and cute . . . for about a week.
- Pale colours add space, dark colours draw things in. Reds, oranges and yellows are warm and stimulating; greys, greens and blues are cool and relaxing while pale pink, creams and brown can be restful without being chilly.
- The kitchen can often be hot and sticky, so use cool colours.
- A bathroom is the place to luxuriate in and rehearse your entry for the Eurovision Song Contest, so use warm colours.
- The rule books say you should avoid stimulating colours in bedrooms, well obviously written by a younger man.
- If a brown stain persists in showing, take a colour chart and paint the wall to match the stain—a sandy colour will usually camouflage it. Mind, you need to be sure that it is just an *old* damp area which produced the stain, not a new problem.
- Paint radiators and pipes the same colour as the walls behind them if you want them to be less obtrusive.
- Matt emulsion shows up imperfections less than shinier finishes.

The fashion world dictates a 'colour of the year'—you didn't think all designers stumbled on the same colour by chance did you? We are more manipulated than that. But there are too many people telling us what we can and can't do, so use whatever colour you like in your cottage. It's not the end of the world if a colour doesn't work out. Paint it over and use the poor colour for inside a cupboard or give it to a friend, or sell it to a relative.

Personally, I'm convinced that if you have stripped an old cottage back to basics, it makes sense to use a plain matt emulsion everywhere. It is the cheapest route, even using the best emulsion; it gives the cottage time to 'settle down' and faults can be corrected before you do more elaborate decoration over the years.

Wallpaper

However, I recognise that to many people a cottage means matching duvets, curtains and wallpapers right from the start (don't forget a shelf for the wok) so bowing to the inevitable, let us start the decoration story by considering wallpaper. And the first thing to consider to help your estimating is that it is sold in nominal lengths of 10.05 metres (around 11 yards) and in nominal widths of 530 mm (approximately 21 in). If possible, take samples of carpets, curtains or paint colours with you when choosing wallpaper or borrow a pattern book and browse over it in the cottage. Relate patterns to the size of a room; if you spot a bold design during a visit to a stately home, don't expect it to look so good in a two up, two down.

If in doubt about how many rolls of wallpaper you need, buy an extra one, having established that you can take it back for a refund, if it is returned unopened. Check the reference numbers on wallpaper rolls to see that they are from the same batch and if at all possible, buy *ready pasted paper*. Although you may sometimes need to use extra paste, especially round the edges, the simplicity of using this compared with the old-fashioned sort is so marked that I hope the inventor got himself into an Honours List.

For wallpapering you need a hanging brush, trimming knife, scraper, paintbrush, sponge, scissors, possibly a ruler, a plumbline and chalk. You will need a bucket, paste and another brush if you are not using ready pasted paper; if using the latter it will come with a cardboard trough to hold water. You will also need a table— proprietary pasting tables aren't expensive although an ordinary kitchen table will suffice. One other thing you need is a partner to help because when wallpapering it is absolutely essential to have someone to rage at during frustrating moments.

Most wallpaper shops will have simple leaflets spelling out the ground rules for papering but here are a few points to keep in mind:

- Treat newly plastered walls with size before wallpapering. This is a slightly smelly and messy process but simply involves applying a glue size—which you buy as a powder and add water—over the surface to stop it soaking up water from the paste too quickly before you've had a chance to put the paper in place. As with so many other DIY operations: follow the instructions on the packet.

- Hang ceilings before you paper walls.
- If a paper has a large pattern then line this up on the main feature of the room—such as the chimney breast—and work outwards from there.
- If you are using paste, apply it down the centre of the back of each length of paper then work outwards towards the edges. Make sure the edges are well plastered but try not to get paste on the front of the paper.
- Use a plumbline (you don't have to buy one, something fairly heavy on a length of string will do) and chalk to get a vertical line for your first length of wallpaper—the cottage walls may not be level.
- When you get to light fittings, switch off electricity at the mains, pierce the paper to correspond with the centre of the switch, then make diagonal cuts out to the corners of the switch. Using the backs of scissors, press round the switch, peel away, cut away and then paste up.
- If you are using ready pasted wallpaper (you should be) every roll will have a sheet of simple instructions with it. Follow them! They will tell you to soak a length of paper for a given length of time in the trough supplied then pull the top up slowly and steadily. In theory the water is supposed to drain into the trough but you will find it will also drain into your shoes and over the floor. You may feel it undignified to wallpaper wearing wellingtons but you can at least put newspaper on the floor to soak up the mess.
- Cheap, thin wallpaper may stretch when you hang it unless you are very careful.
- Textured lining papers help to cover uneven ceilings and walls and look gentler when emulsioned than plain plaster but even if you go to the expense and trouble of using such papers, still put the plaster right first.
- Wall fabrics will camouflage uneven surfaces but they are a lot of work and costly.
- If you hang expensive wallpapers or coverings like hessian then make it the last job because it will be difficult to remove spots of paint from them.

On the tiles

Having considered wallpaper, let's quickly look at something else which you can stick on walls—tiles. With patience, tiling is not a difficult DIY job and all the tile manufacturers have clear instruction leaflets. Have patience, take your time and, above all, establish a level base for the work—don't assume an existing item, such as a shelf, is level. Take the same care with vertical lines. Don't try to paint over old tiles in your cottage to rejuvenate them; it is unlikely to be a success. If you are chipping away at old tiles to remove them, wear some form of eye protection. Remember it will be difficult to tile on uneven walls so attend to the plastering before tiling. Tiles will be with you for quite a while, which suggests you should not pick a really way out pattern or colour scheme which will pall after a month or two.

Painting

Now for what, at first sight, is the easiest decorating job of all—painting. Paint is really in the grip of the metric system and is now sold in a range of tin sizes from 250 millilitres up to 5 litres. The latter can be a bit heavy when you are up a ladder and the 2½ litre size may be more convenient (or buy just one of this size, then when it is used wash out the tin and decant from 5-litre tins into it). As the Metrication Board says 'old brushes fit the new tins'. As a rough guide, 5 litres of gloss will cover 75 square metres on non-porous surfaces; 5 litres of emulsion will cover 90 square metres (less if the surface is porous).

Choose the right paint for your particular application, for instance where condensation is common an oil finish paint is preferable to emulsion because it is more water resistant. As I am a messy worker, I try to use non-drip gloss whenever possible.

For walls and ceilings you should use emulsion. This paint is washable but not scrubbable so if you get any dirt on emulsion paint remove it gently with warm, soapy water; if you overdo the scrubbing process you will make a bigger mess than you started with. You will often see very cheap white emulsions for sale but they will prove poor bargains if three coats are needed to do the work of one coat of a better quality product.

Incidentally, don't store emulsion paints where they may freeze. Turn a gloss paint tin upside down when not in use (yes, you do put the lid on first) so that you don't have to break through a skin the next time you open it.

Don't just buy a tin of paint and a brush and merrily start decorating. Plan the work first. Is all the plastering finished? Has the woodwork been sanded down? Have knots in new timber been treated with a knotting compound? Don't leave any of these things until later because they will involve making a mess which may affect your nice new painting. And before you start painting, ask yourself: if you can't see it, why paint? If the sides of two kitchen units are to be screwed together, why waste paint on them?

In your wild enthusiasm you will make the best job of the first room you paint so start with a living room. Protect the floors and threaten children and pets with instant execution if they intrude. Paint the ceiling before the walls; begin with a corner nearest the window and work away from the light. If you are using a roller, first use a brush in places where the roller can't reach then continue with the roller or large brush and paint in bands parallel to the window *across* the room. Work in convenient size strips, say an arm's width across, or whatever you find easiest without getting muscle bound. Before you start the walls, scrape off any splashes you've made while doing the ceiling otherwise they will show as lumps.

Emulsioning walls, even ceilings, is very easy; painting woodwork is less so. Prime new woodwork, then use a proper undercoat. Sand the surface smooth before you put on the final gloss, otherwise any bits will show through. If you have large holes in woodwork, say, where knots have popped out, fill them a layer at a time. If there are several holes in a door where old locks were positioned, remember a door plate may cover them. When painting skirting boards, use a piece of card or hardboard and run it along the floor as you are painting so that you don't mark the floorboards; rest your tin of paint on the same board so that any drips fall on it.

Windows are a nuisance to paint. You can either tape over the glass before painting or use a proprietary paint shield (or a piece of stiff card) to avoid getting paint on it; remove any masking tape as soon as the work is dry—it may be messy to shift if you leave it too long. The other method, which I usually use but which is not in the text books, is to get paint on the glass then scrape it off with a razorblade or chisel later. I don't think it takes much longer and it can be very satisfying. Theorists say you should paint window glazing bars first, then the cross rails, then the side verticals, then the window frame itself but if a different order suits you then to hell with the theorists—painting is boring so do anything to make it more relaxing. Care though—I emulsioned 'I love you' in large letters on a blank wall for my wife (I'm just a sentimental old fool really) but it showed through the next coat and I got some very strange looks from a man who came to read the meter the next day.

Paint fumes are extremely allergenic (in other words, they get up your nose) and asthma sufferers should take great care. If your children suffer, don't expose them to too many fumes; keep a room well ventilated. Sufferers should take the same care when sanding down—use a smog mask with a changeable lining. You can also use the mask when you rob banks to pay for the renovation.

Wedge doors open so that they don't swing about when you are painting them and, if you feel you may run out of time, paint door edges first so that they will be dry when you come to close the doors.

Never overthin a paint too much or spread it too far—it is tempting to do this if you are in danger of running out. If you thin a paint too much it will look weak against the rest and, worse, will run all over the place, not least down your arms. If you find the paint you are using is rather runny, tie a cloth round the handle of the brush to catch some of it before it covers you.

Every so often during your decorating take time out for a cleaning session—take up old newspapers and generally freshen the place up but don't sweep a room while paint is still wet, of course. When you have finished your painting session, take the trouble to clean your brushes. If you are using emulsion paint, simply wash out your brush or roller under a tap, taking care with a brush to separate the bristles with your fingers so that the paint is removed from the top of them. After using oil-based paints, work the brush vigorously up and down in a solution of water and washing powder, repeat with a fresh solution then rinse in warm water and shake dry. My excellent typist points out that washing-up liquids are better than powder because there are no granules and from personal experience claims that lemon ones are best of all. If cleansing proves very difficult after using oil-based paints, you will need a paint cleaner, washing out afterwards with soap and water. If you are using a roller, clean out the corrugations on the tray as well.

Wash off an emulsion tin at the same time as you clean the brush. Fix the lid firmly and hold the case under the tap and use the brush to wash the paint out of the channel round the lid. It will make the tin more pleasant to use next time. A small quantity of paint left in a tin is likely to dry out in storage so transfer it to a smaller tin or screw-top jar.

When you've cleaned your brushes and tins, clean yourself and use a hand lotion if your hands are very dry; I can hear guffaws from the

Figures 86 and 87. *Just as a beard can cover a multitude of chins, so a door plate can camouflage at least some of the marks on a stripped door where old locks and keyholes have been. Simple locks like the one here provide very little security and are more suitable for outhouses.*

building trade but the Building Regulations don't say that renovation work has to be unnecessarily unpleasant.

You will see dramatic results from your painting but it will take time. As an incompetent DIYer it takes me about one hour to prepare and paint an average cottage wall; longer for ceilings because I get nose bleeds.

Finally, one piece of advice given to me by an old Yorkshire lady as I sweated over the front windows of our cottage—make sure you put the paint on the right way up.

Flooring

If possible attend to floor coverings before adding any furniture to a cottage because it will be much easier to move around. A cheap and effective floor covering for a cottage can be the original floorboards, sanded then sealed. Loose rugs scattered about will be cheaper than fitted carpets although, unless they are strategically placed, life can be a bit uncomfortable in cold weather if you step on wood rather than wool.

Cork flooring can blend well with an old cottage but take care that it is sealed properly—the surface must be clean. Cork tiles may fade if exposed to bright sunlight.

Tiling was used for the surfaces of walls and floors in Egypt as long ago as 4000 BC so you won't be breaking any new ground if you use it in your cottage. By 900 AD decorative wall tiles had become common in Persia, Syria and Turkey and as transport and communications improved, tiles moved westwards and were eventually traced to Chalfont St Giles. Unglazed floor tiles need little maintenance and can be kept clean simply by sweeping and washing with warm water with a neutral detergent in it, but tiles are far less kind to crockery dropped on them than cork.

Your most likely choice of floor covering for a cottage will be one of the vinyl materials available in countless qualities and patterns. They should be placed over a good surface, so if you have irregular floorboards put hardboard over them (rough side up) fixed in place with panel pins. Laying vinyl flooring is not difficult for the DIYer with patience; you need a good pair of scissors or sharp knife, a straight edge, a ruler and the appropriate adhesive. The vinyl will lay easier if you leave it unrolled in a warm room for a while because this will make it more pliable. Don't lay vinyl directly on to floors which have been treated with a preservative (say, against woodworm); put a barrier down first. Steel yourself to take the time to make a neat fit round basins and other fixed items and don't cheerfully **measure** the dimensions of a room then start cutting—check that the **corners of** the room are at right angles first; they may not be in an old **cottage.**

If you settle for carpet as a floor covering, you still **need a** reasonable surface so, once again, nail hardboard over very **uneven** floorboards. Hair felt underlay somehow seems old fashioned, although many experts still prefer it to foam material; the latter is much easier to lay, but it leaves you with a strong smell of rubber on your hands—use gloves when laying it. Other points about carpets? Well, fitted carpets mean fewer edges to trip over; carpet tiles can be swopped around to relieve wear in busy places; carpets should last three times as long as curtains so choose them with three times the care and keep in mind (particularly if you are holiday letting) that plain carpets will show stains more than patterned ones.

Furnishing

Having decorated the cottage and sorted out floor coverings, you can now bring in the furniture. Do consider the use which will be made of the place before furnishing it—for instance, a formal dining room in a holiday cottage may be under-utilised so furnish to allow the room to be used for other activities by using a gate-legged table which can be tucked out of the way.

A tiny room in a cottage will look even smaller if you clutter it with furniture; you are planning a place to live in, not a museum. Before buying furniture, do check that you will actually be able to get it through doors and up narrow stairs. A Habitat catalogue, although perhaps rather clinical, is useful as a guide to prices and, when furnishing, don't turn your nose up too quickly at the mass-producers like MFI; we have found their chairs strong enough to withstand hectic holiday letting.

Don't be afraid of DIY furniture-making because it is fairly easy with modern materials. Buy your faced chipboard where you can get it cut because you should then be sure of getting straight edges and the right angles. Plan carefully to get the maximum number of pieces out of a sheet, keeping in mind where you will need finished edges because iron-on plastic edging looks less tidy. Old chests of drawers fetch little or nothing at auctions and can often be cut about and built-in, with old tops hidden under new ones; look for semi-modern or nondescript drawer units for this purpose because ones with bun handles fit to be stripped fetch silly figures (at least silly if you consider that you can never be quite sure what you will find when they come out of the caustic tank). Old wardrobes fetch even less than drawers at auctions and when broken up make much cheaper shelves than can be obtained by buying new wood. Building your own furniture may be the best, or only, way of making the maximum use of awkward spaces in a cottage.

If you have a recess in a bedroom which is not big enough to house a wardrobe, put a stout shelf across it four or five feet off the ground with a hanging rail underneath; fix curtain tracking to the front edge and make a 'curtain' to draw across in front of your warden's uniform as it hangs there. If you use materials to match existing curtains or bedspreads then the unit should blend in well.

If space is limited, a convertible bed settee will be useful in a cottage although with some of the double ones both partners do tend to roll into the middle (so who's complaining?). If you need a degree in bridge engineering to convert a settee into a bed, forget it. A 'Z' bed is useful, almost essential in fact if you are using the cottage for holiday letting, and if you are really short of space then bunk beds or fold-up wall beds may solve the problem but do get reasonably-sized ones; don't inflict children's sizes on adults.

Fitted covers will brighten old chairs and settees but don't buy

Figure 88. *Cottages should be furnished in character. Note the hanging chains covering a radiator.*

Figure 89. *A simple home-made bedroom unit using a chest of drawers bought for £1 at an auction and re-painted, together with a wardrobe cut from sheets of Contiboard. The brightness of the picture is not poor photography but an attempt to conceal a gap between the sliding door and the side of the 'robe'.*

them if the basic furniture is too tired, it will be false economy.

By the time you have stood for hours at auctions, you may be losing some of your enthusiasm for furnishing but dream your impossible dream just a while longer and sort out things like appropriate lampshades. If you need to fit strong bulbs to brighten a dark cottage then, to avoid fire risk, be sure that the shades will take the wattage.

Just as you should pay attention to lampshades, so should you take care in your choice of curtain tracking. If a window is small then the tracking should be wide enough for open curtains to clear the window to let in the maximum amount of light. You should be able to dispense with dust-gathering pelmets if you buy modern curtain tracking and you can obtain special tracking for net curtains which looks a little more elegant than the traditional lengths of stretched wire. Buy tracking where spare parts are available in case you need extra hooks or ends.

If you wish to increase the apparent width of a room then emphasising something like a curtain rail will help. However, before you rush for curtains, consider whether a roller blind would not be more appropriate, particularly in a kitchen where it can be rolled up out of the way of cooking splashes.

If you do fit curtains, remember that you may have to live with the pattern for several years, so don't choose anything too strident. Personally, I hate velvet curtains because they smack too much of Scarlet O'Hara and brothels (I'm only going by what my friends tell me, of course). A patterned carpet plus patterned curtains, plus patterned wallpaper? Too much, too much.

Wallpapers and fabrics to designs by William Morris usually blend well with cottages, perhaps because he mostly chose creams, pinks and browns. Incidentally, Mr Morris, whose name you are likely to run into quite often, lived from 1834 to 1896; he disliked change and said in a plea for the revival of handicraft: 'As a condition of life, production by machine is altogether an evil'. I bet he believed in Real Ale too.

The weight of curtain fabric you choose will determine whether a lining is needed and remember that if a material has to be dry cleaned it will be more expensive in the long run than one which can be home washed.

One final tip (from the heart) on decorating and furnishing: devote a planned session to 'putting things up'. Countless shelves as well as holders for toothbrushes, toilet rolls and towels will need to be fixed; get the right sized drill bits, screws, screwdrivers and plugs and methodically work your way round the cottage putting everything in its place.

15

Gardens

By the time you finish decorating your cottage, your interest and energy may be flagging but force yourself to plan the garden and find time to sort out the outside area in general.

The first thing to do may be to dispose of the inevitable debris which will have accumulated during the renovation. You can burn timber but there may also be paint tins, water butts, old windows and so on. If you have used a builder he will probably have quoted to leave the place 'clean and tidy', if so pester until he does (builders lose interest in a place towards the end of the work just like we lesser mortals). You should have kept an eye on top soil while any drains and so on were being dug and made sure it was replaced. Find out where the nearest rubbish tip is if you have to dispose of rubbish yourself, or hire a skip. Don't get rid of rubble until you are certain you don't need it as hard core.

Having tidied up generally, you now have to plan for something which was probably not invented when your cottage was built: a car. You don't need planning permission for a hard standing area for a car, provided it is used primarily for a private vehicle and provided the hard standing is constructed in your garden. However, you *do* need planning permission to construct a means of access, such as a path or driveway, to the road unless the access is to an unclassified road and complies with other conditions. It is all explained in the DOE booklet 'Planning Permission—A Guide for Householders'. The consent of the highway authority should also be obtained if your means of access involves crossing any footways or the verge of a road; this consent should really be sorted out at the purchase stage. For safety reasons, the local authority will insist on clear sight lines at the access point, which will probably mean hacking back hedges; if your cottage is on a dodgy stretch of road, consider if there is enough space on your land to turn round so that you can drive out forwards. A strategically

Figure 90. *The cottage shown in* Figure 5 *looks quite respectable towards the end of a renovation; with the ground cleared of rubble, it is time to tackle the garden.*

placed mirror may make for a safer exit if your cottage is on a difficult stretch of road and, as well as helping you, may encourage passing motorists to slow up.

Use paving slabs, rubble (which can be concreted later) or simple gravel as a driveway for a car; top dress gravel to stop weeds.

Concreting may be off-putting but really it is only a case of mixing appropriate ingredients in the right quantities and putting them in the right place. In fact, if you use ready mixed concrete, you don't even have to mix the aggregate, cement and water yourself—but you do have to plan carefully so that the ready mixed is put in place before it sets at the end of the drive as a silent monument to your lack of planning. Of the countless booklets available to the DIY man, 'Concrete round the House' and 'Concrete in Garden Making' both published by the Cement and Concrete Association are among the most informative and helpful. However, don't get so carried away with concrete that your cottage ends up with all the charm of a modern New Town centre—you bought the cottage to get away from horrors like that didn't you?

Garages

Having got the car on to your land, your next job may be to protect it. If so, carports don't normally require town and country planning approval unless they are over 1,750 cubic feet in volume or will encroach in front of the beloved building line. However, they do need approval under the Building Regulations; similar guidelines apply to garages.

Take care over the choice of a garage for an old cottage. Timber ones perhaps blend best but don't last as long as those of other materials. A modern concrete garage may jar, and even up-and-over garage doors may clash with an old property. The ideal would be a garage made of similar brick to the cottage with wooden doors but this would probably be the most expensive. All up to you.

Paths

Having catered for a car, ponder on pedestrians and plan your paths. Routes for paths will follow naturally from the use a garden gets. Try not to make them too formal and straight, although if you weave them about all over the place people will simply cut corners across your garden. If you have the patience, bricks laid on their sides make very elegant paths, more in keeping with a cottage than modern machine cut concrete blocks. If you don't use bricks, consider old slabs. You won't make patterns with modern multi-coloured slabs, will you?

Figure 91. *Vehicular access to this cottage was originally to the right of the tree with cars aiming for the front door. A new entrance was made to spare land at the side of the cottage, leaving a better garden layout.*

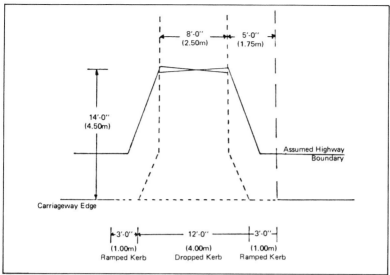

Figure 92. *Your local authority will specify access details along these lines to provide safe sight lines.*

Boundaries

Just as you should have sorted out rights of way when you bought your cottage, so the position over walls and fences should be unambiguous. Liaise with neighbours if there is any doubt over the position of fencing and instead of just referring to tiny plans, sort out fence runs *on site* if necessary. A plan is too small to give a proper guide. You may find there is some clause like this built into the purchase of your cottage:

> **Fencing**. The Purchasers will erect and maintain a suitable fence between points A and B, as indicated by 'T' marks. A gateway will be incorporated in the fence to allow use of the pedestrian right of way 3(b) below. A fence, with gate, will be erected between points C and D and the purchaser will pay for this up to a maximum of £50 and will be responsible for the future maintenance.

At least that was quite specific. Don't worry too much about exact timing stipulations—we were supposed to put up that fence within three months; in fact nine months went by without any hassle. We deliberately left one fence down because neighbours were working on their cottage and we would have impeded their access.

Friends in Ireland had their garden staked out by the local council as part of a road widening process. They crept out during the night and moved the stakes 3 feet further out but the fence was finally found

Figure 93 (Above). *Use natural local stone for terraces where available; this is in the Cotswolds.*

Figure 94 (Below). *If you have to rebuild a wall, keep it in character; the new section here has flint panels to match the older wall to the right.*

to be in exactly the right place. Why? Because the council had pinched 3 feet too much in the first place.

Normally, you don't need planning permission for a fence or wall provided the structure is not more than 1 metre high if it runs along the boundary adjoining a road used by traffic, or 2 metres high elsewhere, provided again that it does not obstruct, in such a way as to cause danger, the view of people driving by. However, there may be clauses imposed by the vendor when you bought the place but if, on reflection, such clauses seem unduly onerous, try ignoring them and see if the vendor bothers to take any action against you.

Choose fences with care. Consider whether a fence is just a boundary marker or whether it also has to protect you against the wind or local eyesores. Very heavy close boarded fences can look offputting and clash with traditional cottages; iron fencing is traditional and long lasting but very expensive. Plastic fencing is maintenance free but may not hold its colour too well and will rattle unless mounted firmly. A cheap fence can be made from lengths of wire strung between simple posts.

If you have the ground, a ha-ha will make an excellent boundary and blend the cottage into its surroundings (as well as proving a conversation piece). As if you didn't know, a ha-ha is a ditch with one vertical side—your side—and one sloping side. Animals and kids can gambol down the slope without hurting themselves but won't be able to clamber up the vertical face on to your flowerbeds. Because all this happens below ground level, a ha-ha will give you an uninterrupted view from your cottage.

Most other fencing is not too difficult to erect by yourself although it will be straighter and firmer if you get a local farmworker, used to fencing, to help. Note yet again the assumption that a cottage will be near a farm, ie, in the country; if yours is just behind the Albert Hall, perhaps you've bought the wrong book?

If you are erecting a wooden fence, do use galvanised or sheridised nails and protect the wood with a preservative like creosote; the length of service partly depends on the degree of penetration, so brush it on generously. Do the work on a warm, dry day when the wood itself is dry and absorbent—not unnaturally, damp wood won't absorb the creosote. Greatest protection is needed where the timber is in contact with the ground and particularly at ground level itself (incidentally posts should have at least one-third of their length in the ground). Remember that treated timber will be very difficult, if not impossible, to paint later and do avoid splashing plants and shrubs or for that matter your hands with creosote (wear gloves). The effect of creosote on

Figure 95 (Left). *Not a pretty sight. Get rid of clutter like this.*

Figure 96 (Below). *Fencing panels like these need to be properly supported and well treated with preservative. A patio is still to be laid in front of these cottages and the builder has left rubble to be used as hardcore.*

Figure 97 (Below right). *The fuel store shown in the plan in* Figure 71 *being bricked up to extend the kitchen, with the closet retained as a store.*

grass is so dramatic that I once marked out the plan of a bungalow on a green plot just using creosote and a small brush.

Two final points on fencing:

- If droppings indicate that you have to keep out rabbits, then you will need to put a wire fence several inches down into the ground. Or buy a gun.
- Don't forget you will need somewhere to tie the ends of a clothes line unless you use a rotary one, which should be cemented into the ground otherwise the wind may blow it over.

Over the years your cottage may have accumulated a ramshackle cluster of corrugated sheds; if possible scrap them. I once tried to burn a collection down to save time and nearly set the adjacent cottage on fire. Stupid and not recommended.

You will not need planning permission for a new shed or greenhouse provided it is not too high or blocks the view to the danger of people using nearby roads. Of course, if your cottage has a traditional outside throne room you may not need a shed becuse you will be able to use it as a store if you add a new bathroom. If you set out to buy a shed I hope you won't need me to tell you not to be over-influenced by 'free floor' offers (who else do they think is paying for it?). Compare like with like, get catalogues and, if possible, see erected sheds in garden centres. If you assemble a shed yourself, take the trouble to prepare and paint or

treat the timber properly; it will be less easy to do when the shed is full of odds and ends. Considering the chemicals you are likely to need around the garden, do put a shelf high up in the shed for them and have them clearly labelled (not kept in lemonade bottles) so that there is no danger to children.

As we have been considering various structures, it is perhaps worth mentioning that you need planning permission to put a flagpole or radio mast in a garden because in planning law either will count as a building structure. You do not need planning permission to keep a caravan or boat in your drive or garden, provided it is for your own enjoyment and simply parked there when not in use; if you wanted to use the van to live in then you would have to apply for planning permission. Some authorities have special local powers to prohibit the parking of caravans and boats in front gardens; I think they should all have because vans can look an eyesore and be an inconvenience to neighbours.

By the way, you don't need planning permission for a porch (which may give you extra storage and will reduce draughts) provided the floor area is not more than 2 square metres; no part of the porch is more than 3 metres above ground level and no part of the porch is less than 2 metres from any boundary between your garden and a road or public footpath. From my experience, not all councils are clear on the rules about porches, so you may have to argue. A porch must harmonise with a cottage; a modern all-glass, flat roofed affair could look absurd on a traditional cottage.

Having sorted out car access, paths and sheds, it is now time to consider the garden itself. This is not intended to be a gardening book (library shelves are full of them) but here are just a few random points to be considered:

- Remove valuable plants, roses and so on at the start of your renovation. Like it or not, builders will need dumps for material and while putting in drains they will tear up a lot of garden.
- Keep a garden notebook, perhaps at the back of a general record book for the cottage, noting what you planted when, whose seeds were used and so on.
- Decide how much time, energy, enthusiasm, skill and money you have before planning how elaborate to make the garden.
- Don't hack the garden about too soon, get a feel for the cottage and its surroundings first.
- Caution: don't rush to fell trees—it takes years to grow one and only minutes to cut one down. If a tree is protected by a tree

preservation order (TPO), you will normally need to obtain local authority consent. If you live in a conservation area you must notify the local authority before felling or lopping any trees; if in doubt, check with your local planning department.

- Prune existing items hard then see the effect before deciding to rip things out—shrubs left unpruned by previous owners may flourish.
- Plan where you are going to keep dustbins (preferably hidden behind a hedge or fence).
- Decide just how big a garden you can handle. If there is too much land with your cottage, consider allowing some of it to run fairly wild, perhaps rough cutting it a couple of times during a season, or let a neighbour keep a pony on it (the happiest solution we've found to the problem).
- Consider viewlines from the cottage when planning a garden. Don't put colourful plants where you will never see them from inside. Most garden plans are drawn from above but surely these can only be of use for parachutists and balloonists, so consider the view you will have from each window of your cottage.
- Make a reasonably accurate scale plan of the garden area. When you study it with a nursery catalogue to hand showing planting distances, you will be able to work out how many of each plant you will need to fill a particular area.
- If you are new to gardening then be prepared for surprises and disappointments. With one cottage, we split the ground into two, carefully grass seeded one half according to the instructions on the pack and rotovated the other half and left it rough for vegetables; this half turned itself into much the better lawn.
- Avoid tall trees or bushes close to windows. Study gardening catalogues for information of the final height of trees and shrubs before planting them.
- If you have not visited a garden centre recently, do so before planning too lavish a layout because some of the prices may frighten you.
- Keep a garden in sympathy with its neighbours. If you are in a terrace of four cottages and three have privet hedges, an open plan garden in front of yours will jar (open plans will rarely be in keeping with cottages anyway).
- A cottage garden should not be too formal. Gardens for cottages

were working gardens designed to produce food and flowers—
don't turn them into refined formal settings.

- If you are using a cottage for holiday letting or simply as a
  second home then design the garden to be easy to maintain.
- Make use of levels in the garden when planning, eg use humps
  for rock gardens; try to make the garden an extension of the
  cottage.
- Watch where the sun falls before planning patio areas.
- Test soil acidity before you get too far with the choice of plants;
  simple test kits are available.
- An artificial well? With a plastic thatched capping? Well . . .
  don't forget the gnomes to guard it.
- You want nice crisp vegetables? Go to a deep freeze store
  unless you are a keen gardener; use your weekends at the
  cottage to refresh the soul not the soil.
- Don't use bowling green quality seed or turf if a lawn will have
  heavy use; buy a coarser mixture.
- Remember the length of time a flower blooms is as important as
  how brightly it does so. Three months of colour are better than
  three weeks.
- A garden pond may be dangerous for toddlers—a sandpit will
  be a delight.

All that started out as just a few notes but rather rambled on. My
apologies.

One final point: it will be cheaper in the long run to get good quality,
traditional garden tools. Auctions often have bundles of all the things
you will need which sell for a fraction of the new price; a good pickaxe
will be an essential item. Incidentally, get spades and shovels small
enough so that your wife and children can use them.

16

Revenue from Your Cottage

After several chapters telling you how to spend money on your cottage, this one deals with how to reverse the cash flow. If the cottage is elaborate or has a splendid garden, I suppose you could open the place to the public or flog flowers from the front, but these methods are not likely to make much impression on your bank balance so, if the cottage is a second home, you may decide to let it. Now I know only bad landlords and brothel keepers get the bad publicity but, as a result of their activities, society seems to regard a private landlord as some sort of monster and certainly fair game for social workers and tenants with half a voice. Over the years I have taken five cottages which were lying derelict and turned them into pleasant places to live or holiday in. Countless other cottage owners have done the same. Are we really so anti-social?

The main problem over letting is the political uncertainty with some politicians committed to the eventual elimination of private sector renting; really you need a political crystal ball to decide whether residential renting is a secure long-term business. If you do, remember that once you have a permanent tenant in your property, it will lose two-thirds of its value—which is why if one of a pair of cottages has a tenant in it, it will be for sale at only a fraction of the price of the one vacant. Tenancies may be passed on within a family; other tenants may cram friends into your cottage and the most reasonably-looking people will appear as down-trodden martyrs (with you as the villain) if they apply to have what you consider a fair rent, reduced.

The position has been eased a little for landlords by the introduction under the 1980 Housing Act of shorthold tenancies. Briefly, a shorthold letting must initially be for a fixed term of between one and five years. During the agreed period the tenant is fully protected so long as he doesn't break the conditions of the tenancy. At the end of the agreed period you have the right to repossession if you want.

Shorthold applies only when the landlord and tenant do not live in the same house or flat. Different rules apply to lettings by resident landlords (for these, get hold of DOE Housing Booklet number 4 'Letting Rooms in your Home').

For a letting to qualify as a shorthold, you as the landlord must fulfil the shorthold conditions as follows:

- The letting must be for a fixed term of between one and five years which cannot be brought to an end earlier by you unless the tenant breaks the conditions of the tenancy.
- The letting must be to a new tenant, ie, you can't swing an existing tenant to the shorthold system.
- Before the tenancy is granted you must give the tenant a notice *in the form laid down by law* (the shorthold notice) so that the tenant knows he is being offered a shorthold tenancy.
- For shortholds in Greater London either a fair rent for the dwelling must already be registered by the Rent Officer or you must obtain a certificate of fair rent before the grant of the tenancy and an application for registration of a fair rent must be made not later than 28 days after the start of the tenancy.
- For shortholds *outside* Greater London which commence on or after 1 December 1981 the registration of a fair rent by the Rent Officer is not compulsory. This means that you and your tenant can agree on the rent to be charged without reference to the Rent Officer, unless a fair rent has already been registered. However, this does not affect the right of either landlord or tenant to apply at any time for the registration of a fair rent by the Rent Officer if he wishes. Once a fair rent is registered, even if it was registered during a previous tenancy, it cannot be increased until such time as a higher rent is registered. If the landlord pays the rates he may, however, pass on increases in rates to the tenant as they fall due.

If you fail to comply with the shorthold conditions then your tenant may get a fully protected Rent Act tenancy but if the conditions are complied with, the tenant has Rent Act protection during the fixed term only.

If the shorthold tenant fails to pay rent or is in breach of other obligations under the tenancy agreement, you can apply for possession during the fixed term, otherwise you must follow the appropriate procedure when the term expires. Not more than three months before the tenancy expires you must give the tenant at least three month's notice in writing of your intention to apply to the court for possession. If the tenant does not leave by the date on which the notice says that you will be applying to the court, you may apply to the court for possession. That application must be made not later than three months later than the date when you said you would be making the application; if you fail to apply within that period then you will have to serve a new notice!

Cheer up because if you fulfil all the shorthold conditions, the court has no power to refuse an order for possession. However, if you fail to give notice by the end of the fixed term then the tenant will be entitled to stay on for a further year under the shorthold. You will then only be able to serve notice nine months after the beginning of the additional year.

It is all spelt out in detail in the DOE Housing Booklet number 8 'Shorthold Tenancies'. There are two further snags:

1. A government could wave a magic wand overnight and turn shorthold tenants into permanent ones.
2. As shorthold tenancies have to be for a minimum of one year they won't help you to put a tenant in a holiday cottage for, say, six winter months.

In general, apart from shorthold tenancies the tenant of a landlord who does not live in the same dwelling has security of tenure—in order to get possession the landlord has got to apply to the court for an order, which will be granted only if the court thinks it reasonable. Grounds for possession could include non-payment of rent and other breaches of the terms of the agreement, but do remember that in any dispute sympathy may be with the tenant, not you the landlord.

If you buy a cottage for retirement then let it with a view to occupying it at your retirement later (and you make this clear at the time of letting) then the court must make an order for possession in your favour. Bear in mind that you must take an order for possession in court, you can't use force to eject tenants. Nor for that matter can you use force to eject squatters (however tempting it may be) so turn to your solicitor instead.

If you hit problems over letting, the Small Landlords Association is active in defending the rights of owners; as they point out, a let which is a *genuine* holiday let gives the occupants no rights whatsoever and this is the most sensible area to look for revenue (unless you are in an area where you can let to foreign servicemen who you can be sure will eventually go home). However, you must be *genuine* in letting for holidays because if the let is a sham (ie, it is a pretend holiday let but is really permanent) then it becomes a tenancy and the occupants have the right to stay and to demand a fair rent (on a long-term basis, of course, your weekly holiday rent may not be considered 'fair').

Under the law, 'where the purpose of the tenancy is to confer on the tenants the right to occupy the dwelling house for a holiday', the accommodation is excluded from the category 'protected tenancies'. Thus if the holidaymaker refuses to leave at the end of the letting period, you have recourse to law—you mustn't march in with staves. Illegal eviction is a criminal offence, as is harassment.

Of greater concern is the problem of letting properties out of season where it might be difficult to find weekly lets for tourists but you can perhaps find a tenant for a longer period—perhaps someone who wants to hide away to write a book. Once a pattern of genuine holiday lets is established you can then do an off-peak let for a maximum of eight months—but you must go through the right procedure and you can have difficulty in getting vacant possession at the end of the period. However fervently people promise to leave at the end of March, if something goes wrong with their plans then you have problems and may have to go to court. Once an off-peak holiday let is over you must re-establish a pattern of genuine holiday lets before you can do an off-peak let. One danger is that some letting agencies simply let on a series of eight-month lets; if this happens any of the occupants could demand protection under the Rent Act.

An example of the damage this uncertainty over letting can cause: our cottage in Yorkshire remained empty for a winter between summer lets yet, reluctantly, we turned away someone in the village who wanted a six months' let, simply because we could not be *positive* of gaining possession by Easter to start holiday letting. The moral is: *get things in writing, go strictly by the letter of the law and always use a solicitor.*

The pity about all this rigmarole is that with cottages used for holiday letting, it would often be worth letting them virtually free of charge during the winter, particularly in cold areas, just to keep them aired if it wasn't for the uncertainty over regaining possession.

On a happier legal note, assuming you have decided to use your cottage for holiday letting, you should not need planning permission if you are letting an existing cottage or house to tourists. Rating authorities have the power to re-rate a cottage from domestic to business rate if it is let for commercial gain for much of the year. However, if your business does not require planning permission, you are not obliged to inform the local council that you are in the holiday business; any initiative on reassessing will have to come from them.

Self-catering accommodation does not require a fire certificate (like an hotel or guest house does) so you won't need to inform the local fire authorities about your activities but needless to say, that does not absolve you from the responsibility of using your common sense and putting in a fire extinguisher.

Before letting your cottage commercially it is a good idea to let friends or relatives use it for a week or two to shake it down; ask them to list anything missing, such as an all-important bottle opener. They should also be the ones to test whether milk is delivered and, during their stay, they should establish if local shops will let your future tenants order goods in advance; if so include the information in the literature you send to people. You could even offer friends with particular skills a given number of weeks of holiday use free in return for a certain amount of work on the cottage during the renovation.

About one-sixth of holidaymakers in Britain use self-service accommodation so there are plenty of people for you to aim at with your renovated cottage; you need to decide whether to try to reach them yourself or through an agent, or some combination of the two. The advantages of using letting agents are that you don't have to do any advertising; there is little hassle; there are few phone calls; you are guaranteed your money and above all, there is a third party involved in the negotiations between you and your tenants. The disadvantages are that you become less involved and, theoretically, earn leass.

Whether you are using an agent or advertising your cottage yourself, do describe the property accurately and if anything, *understate* rather than exaggerate its charms; some people are happy with a simple property and won't necessarily be put off if yours comes into this category. Warn people against bad stairs, ponds or other things that could be dangerous to the old or children. State the approximate age of the cottage and generally do all you can to give holidaymakers a realistic picture.

Some letting agencies will want exclusive rights during the peak months, others may 'buy' the cottage from you, guaranteeing you a certain revenue. Most will charge a small fee for putting your cottage on their books, perhaps plus a small charge for including a photograph brochure. I've only got practical experience of one agency, Taylings in Godalming, and the reason for my limited experience is that I have been totally satisfied with the service they provide. With Taylings, you let them know by the end of August what rent you want for the various weeks in the following year (they then add their percentage) and when their brochure is published later in the year, they have two ways of handling bookings. Under one, you let them handle all bookings without prior reference to you so if you want to use your cottage

Terms and Availability

* Bookings are from Saturday to Saturday and commence at 3:00p.m. on the day of arrival and end at 10.30a.m. on the day of departure.

* A deposit of one-third of the total rental is required at the time of booking.   The balance should be sent a minimum of three weeks before the beginning of your holiday, at which time you will be sent details of where to get the key, etc.   If you are booking less than four weeks before the start of your holiday, then please send the full amount.

* A booking, when confirmed, constitutes a contract which makes you liable for the full rental if you cancel your holiday for any reason.   You may care to take out an appropriate holiday insurance policy to protect yourself;   many schemes are available.

* Electricity is charged for by a slot meter which takes 50p coins.

* Charges for weeks beginning on the Saturdays listed:

January:	3 £30;	10 £30;	17 £30;	24 £30;	31 £30
February:	7 £30;	14 £30;	21 £30;	28 £30	
March:	7 £30;	14 £30;	21 £30;	28 £30	
April:	4 £30;	11 £44;	18 £44;	25 £44	
May:	2 £44;	9 £44;	16 £44;	23 £44;	30 £44
June:	6 £50;	13 £50;	20 £50;	27 £70	
July:	4 £70;	11 £75;	18 £75;	25 £75	
August:	1 £75;	8 £75;	15 £75;	22 £75;	29 £75
September:	5 £50;	12 £50;	19 £50;	26 £50	
October:	3 £44;	10 £44;	17 £44;	24 £44;	31 £30
November:	7 £30;	14 £30;	21 £30;	28 £30	
December:	5 £30;	12 £30;	19 £40;	26 £40	

NB: Weeks crossed through are already booked.

Figure 98 *Part of a simple booking form setting out conditions and weekly charges (which are on the low side).*

yourself you have to let them know. Under the second method they contact you before accepting a booking, ie, you keep the master records; this method means that you can let to friends or dabble in general advertising without reference to them.

If you are new to holiday letting I would recommend you do what we did—work exclusively with an agent for a year, then do a combination of an agent and private advertising. Most agencies will insist that holidaymakers take out insurance when they book so that if they die, fall ill or lose their jobs, the rent owing is still covered; many insurance companies run simple schemes and if you are handling bookings yourself it could be worth including an application form and leaflet with your booking document.

Estate agents in popular areas sometimes handle properties for holiday letting. Agents may add anything up to 25 per cent on top of your letting charge and some offer a service of returnable deposits in the event of breakages. We have never bothered because we find that if people break a glass they usually replace it, often with a more expensive one; in several years of letting we have not been let down by anyone on this score. Perhaps much depends on where you find your tenants and maybe readers of *The Sunday Times* and *The Lady* are well-mannered. When we started we were given earthy advice by a rather jaundiced friend: never let to large parties of Australians at Christmas. But that's surely malicious—a country that has contributed so much to the culture of modern society can't be so bad can it? What d'you mean, yes?

Almost all agencies insist on public liability insurance for a minimum of £100,000 for any one incident. You should note that insurance policies will only cover you for theft involving unlawful entry so you will not be able to claim if holidaymakers steal a valuable antique from your cottage (serves you right for keeping it there in the first place). Insurance is not particularly difficult—we had no trouble in obtaining a third party. Most insurers will stipulate that the water system should be emptied when the cottage is vacant during the winter and some may say that the property should be visited by a neighbour every so often. If you buy a cottage in an area which is strange to you, you will find neighbours more helpful if you take part in the life of the community, getting involved in things like church fetes etc. If you ignore the local folk, you can't expect them to be very sympathetic towards you and any problems with a cottage.

If you decide to let the cottage yourself, you will find Tourist Board publications good places to advertise—as a guide we received over 60 enquiries from a tiny ad in a Yorkshire guide. Remember that

Figure 99. *A reservation form which, together with the terms and conditions shown in* Figure 98, *has sufficient 'legalese' to make people realise that they are making a contract. The dotted lines should be further apart where people have to fill in details. Few holidaymakers seem to specify alternative dates.*

```
Please print!

Please reserve The Cottage, Coxwold for ............weeks from Saturday
.............(date) to Saturday .............(date) at a total rental of
£........... I enclosed the sum of ......... as a deposit.  This is a
minimum of one third of the total rental and I understand that this is non-
returnable and that I am liable for the full rental if I cancel a confirmed
booking.  I confirm that the balance of the rental will be sent 3 weeks before
the start of the holiday.  My party will consist of .... adults and .... children.

I agree that my booking is for a holiday only and I understand that the property
is used as a holiday establishment and will be so used in future.

Name: .......................    Address: ...................................
............................................................................
Telephone: ...................    Signed: ...................................

If the week/s I want are already booked when you receive this form then

    * return my deposit                          )   Please delete
    * book the following date/s instead:...................)   as appropriate
```

although most holidays are taken in July and August, the main time for *booking* them is January to March, so that's when you need to be doing your advertising but watch this timing carefully because people do seem to be booking later and later—each year we get two or three people booking on a Friday for a holiday starting the next day. Be a little cautious if this happens—one such person's cheque bounced and their holiday was over before the bank returned it.

We have tried cards in newsagents windows (no response) as well as advertising in *The Observer*, *The Lady*, and *The Sunday Times*. In a test with exactly the same ad in all three, *The Lady*, pulled in 40 per cent more enquiries than the other two at a lower cost. Also, I have to say, the Sunday papers do sell their ad space painfully hard if you phone them; don't be bullied.

Research shows that of people staying four nights or more in any one place, a quarter take their holidays in August, one fifth in July, one tenth in June and September. May is a strange month, we've found that one year a cottage books easily, the next it stays empty. If you find odd patterns like this then adjust your charges accordingly. Around one-third of our tenants come from abroad so if any of your friends make cracks about profiteering landlords, hit them over the head with your Union Jack and point out your contribution to Britain's balance of payments.

Avoid petty restrictions on your property. If you stipulate that you won't accept single week bookings, pets, children, agnostics or whatever, you will simply reduce your revenue through fewer lets. However, don't overload the cottage; the bathroom will get over-booked and there will be heavy wear and tear on the place. Don't try to squeeze an excess number of people in—greedily; we have done this twice and got hurt letters both times. Stipulate, say, four/five people rather than five/six if in doubt.

Having got excited about planning and booking a holiday, people will want efficient service and a proper acceptance of their booking, so get your paperwork organised. Other owners may have different methods but our procedure is as follows:

1. Advertise (remember Tourist Board publications close for press very early). We don't ask for an SAE because it seems nitpicking.
2. In response to enquiries—which come mainly by phone—we send:
   (a) a brief letter
   (b) details of the cottage

    (c) a combined price-list and tear-off booking form (we cross through on the price-list any weeks already booked).

    (d) a Tourist Board leaflet, where available.

3. When a booking is received, we log it on a master record card, kept near the phone ready to deal with enquiries—and send an acknowledgement to the holidaymaker. We bank their one-third deposit.

4. When the balance of a booking is received, we bank the cheque, log it on the record card and send the holidaymaker details of how to find the cottage and where to get the key.

5. When the following year's price list is available, we send it to the previous year's mailing list.

People must be given clear instructions for finding your cottage; they may arrive late, in the dark when it is raining and they may have fractious children with them; if they can find the cottage and gain access quickly then their holiday will get off to a good start. Warn people in your final letter about things like dangerous steps in a garden path. Incidentally, the English Tourist Board has a booklet 'Providing for Disabled Visitors' which is for hotel and guest house proprietors but is equally useful for owners of self-catering places.

It is nice if someone can put a bunch of flowers in the cottage and perhaps light a fire in very bad weather because first impressions are important and if people enjoy a holiday in your cottage, they will tell their friends and you may eventually build up a list of people so that you can cut out national advertising and agents and their commission; there is nothing better than word-of-mouth to build business.

As part of your general treatment of holidaymakers, try to develop links with local shops so that people can order groceries in advance. There must be an emergency contact so that a holidaymaker can get in touch with someone if anything goes wrong. In fact it is worth building up a 'cottage book' which includes a welcome, then details about: electricity, clothes drying, where to put rubbish, when dustmen call, how to work the washer (if any), windows or door locks needing special treatment, babysitters, beaches, sightseeing, churches, local walks, car parking, milk deliveries, newspapers, nearest Post Office, pony trekking, sailing, nearest pubs, shops, garages, early closing and market days and nearest telephone.

If you put a box of information leaflets in a cottage and ask people to add anything they collect during their own explorations, you will find the pile will grow during the season. Once a year throw out timetables and things which are out of date.

WEEK	RENT	BOOKED BY	FORM + DEPOSIT REC'D ACKNOWLEDGE. SENT	BAL. REC'D FINAL INSTRUCTIONS SENT	TOTAL RENT REC'D
MAY 9-16	£50				–
" 16-23	£50	J Smith	£17 4 Feb.	£33 8 April	£50
" 23-30	£50	B. Brown	£17 18March	£33 1 May	£50
MAY 30 -JUNE 6	£60				–
JUNE 6 -13	£60	A Jones	£20 3 Jan	£40 29April	£60

Add helpful information but do *not* decorate the cottage with notices saying don't do this and don't do that; put such instructions (and I recognise there may have to be some) in one place, preferably in 'the book'. If possible, display key information in French, German and Dutch as well as English.

Rentals should include gas, electricity, fuel etc where possible unless there are slot meters for electricity or gas (they should take 50p coins). Don't set slot meters at excessive rates. *By law* a landlord who sells electricity or gas to tenants must not charge more than a maximum resale rate, determined by the Area Electricity Board or British Gas; if you get too greedy you could end up in gaol. (Gas and electricity showrooms should have leaflets setting out the latest regulations.) Even if you don't break the law, just because holidaymakers are paying for gas and electricity does not absolve you from the common-sense approach of lagging the hot water cylinder.

Cottages being let must have an adequate supply of crockery, pots, pans, blankets (or duvets) for the number of people they sleep, but linen is not usually included. However, if you find someone in the area to do laundry, offer linen because it will increase your bookings; it is normal to make an additional charge if linen is offered. Overseas visitors in particular welcome it. Keep in mind that not everyone likes nylon sheets.

Equip the cottage with as many labour-saving devices as possible— housewives don't go on holiday to work. Refrigerators and drying facilities are essential, a spin dryer and microwave will be appreciated, while a washing machine and a TV will attract more bookings. Try to make the equipment foolproof, have clear working instructions for it and have a local maintenance man listed in the cottage for people

Figure 100 (Left). *Keep a simple record like this near to your phone. Write the details on a stiff card so that it will survive a year's wear and tear. The form assumes that acknowledgements are sent on the days cheques are received (they should be). If you 'hold' phone bookings for, say, five days until booking forms are received, then* pencil *in the details, inking them in when the cash arrives;* file *the detailed forms in date order. The taxman will be interested in the final column!*

Figure 101 (Right). *If you need to prepare a sales leaflet before a renovation is completed, a sketch like this may be one answer, although holidaymakers may be a little suspicious—note how the artist has obligingly not noticed the end cottage shown in* Figure 24.

to call in if something goes wrong. Incidentally, people have different ideas on how clean a cooker should be but it will help if you buy one that is easy to maintain.

The inventory for self-catering accommodation, recommended by the English Tourist Board is as follows:

Per bed
3 blankets or 1 continental quilt and cover

1 per person
Pillow
Knife (table & dessert)
Fork (table & dessert)
Spoon (dessert & tea)
Plate (large & small)
Tea cup and saucer
Cereal/soup plate
Tumbler
Egg cup

2 per person
Coathangers

2 per unit
Table spoons
Mixing bowls or basins
Dusters
Ash trays

1 per unit

Kettle	Potato peeler
Teapot	Large fruit dish
Tea caddy	Butter dish
Saucepan and lid (large, medium and small)	Sugar basin
	Tray
Frying pan	Milk jug
Colander	Condiment set (2 piece)
Oven roasting tray	Washing-up bowl
Casserole dish	Dustpan and brush
Carving knife and fork	Broom
Bread knife	Floor cloth
Bread/cake container	Pot scourer/dish mop
Bread and cake plate	Bucket
Bread/chopping board	Mirror
Fish slice	Doormat
Small vegetable knife	Covered kitchen refuse container
Tin opener	
Corkscrew/bottle opener	Fire extinguisher

Do keep in mind that these are *minimum* standards so don't buy the whole lot second-hand at jumbles. Take cutlery as an example; enough basic stainless steel cutlery from, say, Habitat, should not bankrupt you but it will make a lot better impact on guests than ancient bone-handle knives from junk shops. It's the same story with crockery. Don't forget a chip pan, set of basins, poacher, lemon squeezer and large sieve—all unbreakable wherever possible. Stainless steel is not a particularly 'warm' material but it does last so is ideal for bowls, jugs and so on.

Be generous with dustbins otherwise you will be clearing up the bin area every week and don't skimp on doormats or waste paper baskets. A good vacuum cleaner is essential and you should arrange to have windows cleaned during the letting season. And the garden must be properly maintained; it needn't look like Kew but it mustn't be overgrown.

Let neighbours have your name and address and phone number in case the cottage catches fire while your regular cleaner/keyholder is on holiday. (I am assuming in all of this that you may live some way away from your cottage; things will be simpler if you are nearby.)

If you live some distance from your cottage and are using it for holiday letting then the success of the operation will depend on finding someone to look after it for you and clean between lets. Finding this jewel could be difficult because you are only offering an hour or two's work on Saturdays, yet you are imposing a heavy responsibility. The cottage *must* be kept clean and your 'caretaker' must have the wit to cope with burst pipes in winter or harvest mice in summer so it is worth paying well for the peace of mind of having someone sensible in charge; they should be given the key to the electricity slot meter if you have one so that they can pay themselves out of the proceeds.

You need at least three sets of keys—one for you, one for tenants and one for whoever looks after your cottage. Don't make a practice of visiting your cottage while holidaymakers have it booked because it is discourteous to disrupt people's holiday.

If your cottage is simply used by you as a second home, duplicate equipment as much as possible so that you are not short of a vital kitchen tool every time you get there late on a Friday night.

Holidaymakers should normally be asked to turn up between certain hours, say not before 3 pm. They should be asked to leave not later than 10.30 am on the day of departure to allow adequate time for cleaning. Normal lets are from Saturday to Saturday but you will increase your revenue if you can be more flexible. We, for instance, did by taking part-weeks or a weekday to weekday to allow people to use midweek bargain rail offers. Remember you are offering a *service* so make things as easy as possible for holidaymakers.

Incidentally, the greatest demand by holidaymakers is for places which sleep five or six. They should be in full-sized *single* beds—you will reduce your lettings if you have double beds. Bunk beds will be acceptable if full-sized and a spare 'Z' bed is useful and takes up little space. If you have accumulated odd beds from various sources at least try to standardise on matching headboards—not difficult for the DIY man to make.

When you have equipped the cottage think if there are any small things you can add to make that extra difference, such as a patchwork pin cushion with needles and threads etc. Large scale Ordnance Survey maps framed and hung on walls make useful decorations. Small things make a difference: don't use wire coat hangers from cleaners, plastic ones are cheap but add a bit of colour. Have spare electric light bulbs and fuses, a first aid kit and plenty of children's games, jigsaws and books. An added touch is to have a local weekly paper delivered so that people can find out what is going on.

Do bear in mind when furnishing a cottage for letting that skimping will probably cost you more in the long run. If a standard lamp fetches

50p in an auction, you know why don't you? Because it is only *worth* 50p and likely to fall to pieces. You *can* furnish cheaply and well if you have the time to attend enough auctions—dressing tables and wardrobes for instance, rarely fetch more than a pound or two—but try to brighten the place with a few better pieces. Have maintenance-free furniture whenever possible, eg stained wood tables mark, pine ones don't.

I mentioned earlier in the book that it helps to keep jotting things down about the cottage in a notebook. It's worth maintaining the book when you are letting to keep a note of things like the paints used in the cottage so that you can match them later. Keep the paint range simple and perhaps have a shelf or cupboard somewhere in the cottage to store basic essentials for routine maintenance.

However well you furnish and care for your cottage, if you let during the winter people will still expect low rents (except at Christmas and New Year) but they *won't* expect damp so if there is any doubt about the condition of your cottage during the winter, take it off the market.

Bear in mind that holiday letting at coastal areas is seasonal—seaside accommodation is mainly used for beach holidays during school holidays. Letting periods will be longer for cottages inland where people can take general touring holidays. As an example of the sort of occupancy rate you can expect, in East Anglia the Tourist Board reckons you might receive an 80 per cent occupancy rate for about eight months of the year and perhaps 30 per cent for a further three or four months.

Don't forget that all earned income must be declared for tax purposes, which means you need to keep sufficient records to keep the taxman happy. (Letting agencies will be obliged to let the tax people know what you have earned from them.) Right from the start of your renovation, you should retain *all* bills and get into the habit of putting them in a certain place. Write them up in an accounts book (with headings covering repairs, advertising, furniture and fittings etc), then number and file them in case the taxman wants a look later. It may be difficult to get bills if you are buying fireguards and things for 10p a time at jumble sales!

If the letting business is run by your wife, and she has no other income, then there may be a small tax saving by charging the work she does on the cottage but watch you are not claiming that your wife is doing everything if it is clear that it is all being handled by an agency. Your wife has to be paid at a commercial rate, reasonable in relationship to the overall project—she can't charge £100 an hour.

Holiday accommodation is liable to VAT, but if your total letting income is less than the current VAT ceiling (which varies from time to time) then you will be exempt and won't have to add VAT to rents. Agents' commission *will* attract VAT but they will handle this themselves as an add-on item.

As far as the dreaded income tax is concerned, the situation is that, broadly, if the property is let out basically on lets of *less* than 31 days at a time (which is most likely with holiday lets) for at least seven months of the year, the income is treated as being earned income and is put into your overall pot with all your other income. You can offset against rents all the expenses of maintenance, repairs, rates, cost of collecting the rent, accountant's charges, insurance, interest on money borrowed and cleaning. If, after all that lot, you make a loss, you can set that loss against your other income and get a tax repayment. If you make a profit, you are allowed to take out a retirement pension of up to 20 per cent of that profit and obtain tax relief on that pension but, of course, the income sits on top of all your other income. Being earned income, this means that your wife has a share of it and if she is not paying tax then the first £2300-odd is tax free; there is therefore quite an incentive to put these properties in one's wife's name (assuming divorce proceedings are not pending). From the capital gains tax point of view, if you sell the property and purchase another then the capital gain may be 'rolled-over' into the cost of the new property and no capital gains tax is immediately payable.

If the cottage is let for periods of *more* than 31 days then the income is assessed in a separate 'compartment' against which can be set the direct expenses of that income; if you then make a loss the only way that loss can be relieved is against income from the same source. However, you can roll losses forward so that when you have eventually paid off the loan and bought the place, you will still have losses to offset against income. By then, of course, income tax may be so low that all the juggling will have been a waste of time. One can dream.

By the way, there is no capital gains tax charged on death or on non-residents so, if you bitterly resent paying the tax when you sell your cottage, either die or head for Bermuda, whichever you feel will be the warmer. Remember that the first chunk of 'gain' is free of tax and that capital gains tax takes account of any inflationary increases from March 1982 onwards. You don't get tax relief if you keep a place for less than a year but it will probably take you longer than that to buy and renovate a cottage anyway.

Caution: the whole question of tax can become very complicated and the tax people are not fools, so if you have any doubt about income tax, VAT, or capital gains tax (superseded by inheritance tax with effect from March 1986) consult a solicitor or accountant.

For the record, our Yorkshire cottage was bought for £7,400 and sold five years later for £24,000 so there was a reasonable capital appreciation (more important was the capital appreciation our children had of some of the splendours of Yorkshire). However, if you have £24,000 to spare there are better things to do with it than buy property if you want an income—the money would earn more in a bank. Nevertheless, renovating can still be an exciting challenge and anyway, money isn't everything, that's what I always say.

What do you always say?

Useful Addresses

Agrement Board, Lord Alexander House, Waterhouse Street, Hemel Hempstead, Herts HP1 1DH.

British Association of Removers, 279 Gray's Inn Road, London WC1X 8SY; 01–837 3088.

British Ceramic Tile Council, Federation House, Station Road, Stoke on Trent ST4 2RU.

British Ready Mixed Concrete Association, Shepperton House, Green Lane, Shepperton, Middx TW17 8DN.

British Wood Preserving Association, Premier House, 150 Southampton Row, London WC1B 5AL; 01–837 8217.

Builders Merchants Federation, 15 Soho Square, London W1V 5FB; 01–439 1753.

Building Centre Information Service, 26 Store Street, London WC1E 7BS; also in other major towns and cities.

Building Research Advisory Service, Building Research Station, Garston, Watford WD2 7JR; Garston 676612.

The Building Societies Association, 3 Savile Row, London W1X 1AF; 01–437 0655.

Cement & Concrete Association, Wexham Springs, Slough SL3 6PL.

Chipboard Promotion Association, 7a Church Street, Esher, Surrey KT10 8QS.

Copper Development Association, Orchard House, Mutton Lane, Potters Bar, Herts EN6 3AP; Potters Bar 50711.

The Crafts Council, 12 Waterloo Place, London SW1Y 4SU; 01–839 8000.

Department of the Environment, 25 Savile Row, London W1X 2BT.

Fibre Building Board Development Organisation Ltd (FIDOR), 1 Hanworth Road, Feltham, Middx TW13 5AF; 01–751 6107.

Fire Extinguishing Trades Association, 74 Exmoor Drive, Worthing, Sussex BN13 2PJ.

Fire Protection Association, 140 Aldersgate Street, London EC1A 4HY; 01–606 3757.

Glass & Glazing Federation, 6 Mount Row, London W1Y 6DY; 01–409 0545.

Guild of Architectural Ironmongers, 8 Stepney Green, London E1 3JU; 01-790 3431.

Gypsum Products Development Association, 235 Blackfriars Road, London SE1 8NW; 01-248 1661.

34 Palace Court, London W2 4JG; 01–229 2488.

Institution of Electrical Engineers, Savoy Place, Victoria Embankment, London WC2R 0BL; 01-240 1871.

Institute of Plumbing, Scottish Mutual House, North Street, Hornchurch, Essex RM11 1RU; 040 24 72791.

National Cavity Insulation Association, PO Box 12, Haslemere, Surrey; Haslemere 54011.

National Inspection Council for Electrical Installation Contracting, Vintage House, 36 Albert Embankment, London SE1 7TB; 01–582 7746.

The Royal Association for Disability and Rehabilitation (RADAR), 25 Mortimer Street, London W1N 8AB; 01–637 5400.

Royal Institute of British Architects, 66 Portland Place, London W1N 4AD; 01–580 5533.

The Royal Institution of Chartered Surveyors, 12 Great George Street, London SW1P 3AD; 01-222 7000.

Small Landlords Association, Secretary: Miss L Cline, 7 Rosedene Avenue, Streatham, London SW16 2LS; 01–769 5060.

The Soil Association, Walnut Tree Manor, Haughley, Stowmarket, Suffolk IP14 3RS.

TRADA (Timber Research & Development Association) Stocking Lane, Hughenden Valley, High Wycombe, Bucks HP14 4ND.

Further Reading from Kogan Page

Buying and Renovating Houses for Profit by K Ludman and R B Buchanan
How to Cut Your Fuel Bills by Lali Makkar and Mary Ince
Running Your Own Building Business by Kim Ludman
Working for Yourself: The Daily Telegraph Guide to Self-Employment by Godfrey Golzen

Index